John Douglas Borthwick

The Harp of Canaan

Or Selections from the Best Poets on Biblical Subjects. Second Edition

John Douglas Borthwick

The Harp of Canaan
Or Selections from the Best Poets on Biblical Subjects. Second Edition

ISBN/EAN: 9783337277512

Printed in Europe, USA, Canada, Australia, Japan

Cover: Foto ©Lupo / pixelio.de

More available books at **www.hansebooks.com**

THE
HARP OF CANAAN

OR

SELECTIONS FROM THE BEST POETS

ON

BIBLICAL SUBJECTS

BY

REV. J. DOUGLAS BORTHWICK

AUTHOR OF

"*Cyclopædia of History & Geography,*" "*The British American Reader,*"
"*The Battles of the World,*" &c., &c.

SECOND EDITION REVISED AND IMPROVED.

MONTREAL:
PRINTED & PUBLISHED BY GEO. E. DESBARATS,
At the Office of the "Canadian Illustrated News."

1871.

he year of Our Lord one
by REV. JOHN DOUGLAS
riculture.

PREFACE.

OF all tasks which combine dignity with pleasure, and importance with cheering encouragement, there is none surely that can be compared to that of awakening in young people the perception and the enjoyment of poetry. It is the only branch of education in which three quarters of the work is done for us already. Yet, though it be at once the easiest and the most delightful of the teacher's duties, it has been, perhaps, in many instances the most neglected of all. To many, we have no doubt, the undertaking seems visionary and impracticable. Such will admit that it may be good, in an intellectual point of view, to make a child learn verses by heart, and right, in a moral and religious one, that he should be able to repeat hymns and religious poems; but to expect from him sympathy or pleasure in poetry as such, is, in their creed, to expect an impossibility. Hence, perhaps, it is that so little attention has been paid to the quality of the verses contained in books of poetry and elocution from which young people are to learn. Till very lately they were all but made up of the very refuse of the English language. What wonder, then, that children should have confirmed the theory which held poetical enjoyment to be impossible at their age!

If there be no valid objection to addressing the minds of children with poetry, let us study to do so, for there is all imaginable argument in its favour. Poetry is the *safest*, as it is the *highest exercise of the imagination*. The terrors to which that power so naturally does homage are shorn of their direst and most baleful aspects, when they are brought within the realm of beauty. Thoughts of awe will not so readily act as "night fears," when once they have moved "harmonious numbers." And to enjoy poetry at all, is always an exercise, however unconscious, of the intellect; so that by giving the imagination this its best and noblest outlet, we are making it help to strengthen, instead of, as it otherwise might, enfeeble the mind. Last of all, it is through poetry that religious truth most readily finds its way to the heart of "children and child-like souls;" this divine influence it is which enables us to sympathize with holy men of old. Sacred poetry is, after, of course, her creed, sacraments, liturgy, and ministry, the brightest possession of the Church—the richest pasturage of her children; eminently fitted, therefore, for her little ones, who, as yet, require none of her stern discipline; whose minds are all open to its gentle and holy inspiration; ready for truth when so presented to them as that they can livingly apprehend it, but incapable of giving it any cordial reception in the forms of logic, or the loveless antagonism of controversy.

For all these reasons, we say, cultivate in children a taste for poetry. It is hardly a labour to do so; and in as far as it is one, it is nearly sure to be richly rewarded.

J. DOUGLAS BORTHWICK.

June 1, 1871.

THE HARP OF CANAAN.

HISTORICAL INCIDENTS OF THE OLD TESTAMENT.

THE CREATION.

The spacious firmament on high,
With all the blue ethereal sky,
And spangled heavens, a shining frame,
Their great Original proclaim.
Th' unweari'd sun, from day to day,
Does his Creator's power display;
And publishes to ev'ry land
The work of an Almighty hand.

Soon as the ev'ning shades prevail,
The moon takes up the wondrous tale,
And nightly to the list'ning earth
Repeats the story of her birth;
While all the stars that round her burn,
And all the planets in their turn,
Confirm the tidings as they roll,
And spread the truth from pole to pole.

What though in solemn silence all
Move round the dark terrestrial ball?
What though no real voice, nor sound,
Amidst their radiant orbs be found?
In Reason's ear they all rejoice,
And utter forth a glorious voice;
For ever singing, as they shine,
" The hand that made us is Divine."

THE CREATION.

———Meanwhile the Son
On His great expedition now appear'd,
Girt with Omnipotence, with radiance crown'd
Of Majesty Divine; sapience and love
Immense, and all His Father in Him shone.
About His chariot, numberless were pour'd
Cherub, and seraph, potentates, and thrones,
And virtues, wing'd spirits, and chariots wing'd
From th' armory of God, where stand of old
Myriads, between two brazen mountains lodg'd
Against a solemn day, harness'd at hand,
Celestial equipage! and now came forth
Spontaneous, for within them spirit liv'd,
Attendant on their Lord: heaven open'd wide
Her ever-during gates, harmonious sound!
On golden hinges moving, to let forth
The King of Glory, in His powerful Word
And Spirit coming to create new worlds.
On heavenly ground they stood; and from the shore
They view'd the vast immeasurable abyss,
Outrageous as a sea, dark, wasteful, wild,
Up from the bottom turn'd by furious winds
And surging waves, as mountains, to assault
Heaven's height, and with the centre mix the pole.
" Silence, ye troubled waves, and thou deep, peace!"
Said then th' omnific Word; " your discord end : "
Nor stay'd; but on the wings of cherubim
Uplifted, in paternal glory rode
Far into Chaos, and the world unborn;
For Chaos heard His voice. Him all His train
Follow'd in bright procession, to behold
Creation, and the wonders of His might.
Then stay'd the fervid wheels; and in His hand
He took the golden compasses, prepar'd
In God's eternal store, to circumscribe
This universe, and all created things.
One foot He center'd, and the other turn'd
Round through the vast profundity obscure,
And said, " Thus far extend, thus far thy bounds,
This be thy just circumference, O world! "

THE FIRST SABBATH.

HERE finish'd He, and all that He had made,
View'd, and behold all was entirely good;
So even and morn accomplish'd the sixth day:
Yet, not till the Creator, from His work
Desisting, though unwearied, up return'd,
Up to the heaven of heavens, His high abode;
Thence to behold this new created world,
The addition of His empire, how it show'd
In prospect from His throne, how good, how fair,
Answering His great idea. Up He rode,
Follow'd with acclamation, and the sound
Symphonious of ten thousand harps that tuned
Angelic harmonies; the earth, the air
Resounded (thou remember'st, for thou heard'st,)
The heavens and all the constellations rung,
The planets in their station listening stood,
While the bright pomp ascended jubilant.
" Open, ye everlasting gates!" they sung,
" Open, ye heavens, your living doors; let in
" The great Creator from His work return'd
" Magnificent, His six days' work, a world;
" Open, and henceforth oft; for God will deign
" To visit oft the dwellings of just men,
" Delighted; and with frequent intercourse
" Thither will send His winged messengers
" On errands of supernal grace."—So sung
The glorious train ascending: He through heaven,
That open'd wide her blazing portals, led
To God's eternal house direct the way;
A broad and ample road, whose dust is gold,
And pavement stars, as stars to thee appear
Seen in the galaxy, that milky-way
Which nightly, as a circling zone, thou seest
Powder'd with stars. And now on earth the seventh
Evening rose in Eden, for the sun
Has set, and twilight from the east came on,
Forerunning night; when at the holy mount
Of heaven's high-seated top, the imperial throne
Of Godhead fixed for ever firm and sure,
The Filial Power arrived, and sat Him down
With His great Father there; and, from His work
Now resting, bless'd and hallow'd the seventh day,
As resting on that day from all His work.
But not in silence holy kept: the harp
Had work and rested not; the solemn pipe,
And dulcimer, all organs of sweet stop,

All sounds on fret by string or golden wire,
Temper'd soft tunings, intermix'd with voice
Choral or unison: of incense clouds,
Fuming from golden censers, hid the mount.
Creation and the six days' acts they sung :
" Great are Thy works, Jehovah! infinite
" Thy power! what thought can measure Thee, or tongue
" Relate Thee? Greater now in Thy return
" Than from the giant angels: Thee that day
" Thy thunders magnified; but to create
" Is greater than created to destroy.
" Who can impair Thee, Mighty King, or bound
" Thy empire? Easily the proud attempt
" Of spirits apostate, and their counsels vain,
" Thou hast repell'd ; while impiously they thought
" Thee to diminish, and from Thee withdraw
" The number of Thy worshippers. Who seeks
" To lessen Thee, against his purpose serves
" To manifest the more Thy might: his evil
" Thou usest, and from thence createst more good..
" Witness this new-made world, another heaven
" From heaven-gate not far, founded in view
" On the clear hyaline, the glassy sea ;
" Of amplitude almost immense, with stars
" Numerous, and every star perhaps a world
" Of destined habitation; but Thou know'st
" Their seasons: among these the seat of men;
" Earth with her nether ocean circumfused,
" Their pleasant dwelling place. Thrice happy men
" And sons of men whom God hath thus advanced !
" Created in His image there to dwell
" And worship Him; and in reward to rule
" Over His works, on earth, in sea, or air,
" And multiply a race of worshippers
" Holy and just; thrice happy, if they know
" Their happiness, and persevere upright!"
So sung they, and the empyrean rung
With hallelujahs: thus was the Sabbath kept.

GOD VISIBLE IN ALL NATURE.

There lives and works
A soul in all things, and that soul is God.
The beauties of the wilderness are His,
That make so gay the solitary place,
Where no eye sees them; and the fairer forms

That cultivation glories in are His.
He sets the bright procession on its way,
And marshals all the order of the year;
He marks the bounds which Winter may not pass,.
And blunts his pointed fury; in its case,
Russet and rude, folds up the tender germ,
Uninjured, with inimitable art;
And, ere one flowery season fades and dies,
Designs the blooming wonders of the next.

The Lord of all Himself through all diffused,
Sustains, and is the life of all that lives.
Nature is but a name for an effect,
Whose cause is God. . . . One Spirit—His
Who wore the platted thorns, with bleeding brows—
Rules universal nature. Not a flower
But shows some touch, in freckle, streak, or strain,
Of His unrivalled pencil. He inspires
Their balmy odours, and imparts their hues,
And bathes their eyes with nectar, and includes,
In grains as countless as the sea-side sands,
The forms with which He sprinkles all the earth.
Happy who walks with Him! whom what he finds
Of flavour or of scent in fruit or flower,
Or what he views of beautiful or grand
In Nature, from the broad majestic oak
To the green blade that twinkles in the sun,
Prompts with remembrance of a present God.

ADAM'S FIRST SENSATIONS.

As new waked from soundest sleep,
Soft on the flowery herb I found me laid,
In balmy sweat which with his beams the Sun
Soon dried, and on the reeking moisture fed.
Straight toward heaven my wondering eyes I turned,
And gazed a while the ample sky; till, raised
By quick instinctive motion, up I sprung,
As thitherward endeavouring, and upright
Stood on my feet. About me round I saw
Hill, dale, and shady woods, and sunny plains,
And liquid lapse of murmuring streams; by these
Creatures that lived and moved, and walked or flew;
Birds on the branches warbling. All things smiled.;
With fragrance and with joy my heart o'erflowed.
Myself I then perused, and limb by limb

Surveyed and sometimes went, and sometimes ran
With supple joints, as lively vigour led:
But who I was, or where, or from what cause,
Knew not. To speak I tried, and forthwith spake;
My tongue obeyed, and readily could name
Whate'er I saw. " Thou Sun," said I, " fair light,
And thou enlightened Earth, so fresh and gay,
Ye hills and dales, ye rivers, woods, and plains,
And ye that live and move, fair creatures, tell,
Tell, if you saw, how I came thus, how here?
Not of myself! By some great Maker, then,
In goodness and in power pre-eminent:
Tell me how may I know him, how adore,
From whom I have that thus I move and live,
And feel that I am happier than I know."

THE GARDEN OF EDEN.

Southward through Eden went a river large,
Nor changed his course, but through the shaggy hill
Passed underneath engulf'd; for God had thrown
That mountain as his garden mould, high raised
Upon the rapid current, which through veins
Of porous earth, with kindly thirst up drawn,
Rose a fresh fountain, and with many a rill
Watered the garden; thence united fell
Down the steep glade, and met the nether flood,
Which from his darksome passage now appears:
And now divided into four main streams,
Runs diverse, wandering many a famous realm
And country, whereof here needs no account;
But rather to tell how, if Art could tell—
How, from that sapphire fount the crispèd brooks,
Rolling on orient pearls and sands of gold,
With mazy error under pendent shades,
Ran nectar, visiting each plant, and fed
Flowers worthy of Paradise, which not nice Art
In beds and curious knots, but Nature boon
Poured forth profuse on hill, and dale, and plain,
Both where the morning sun first warmly smote
The open field, and where the unpierced shade
Imbrowned the noontide bowers: thus was this place
A happy rural seat of various view;—
Groves whose rich trees wept odorous gums and balm,
Others, whose fruit, burnished with golden rind,
Hung amiable, Hesperian fables true,

If true, here only, and of delicious taste :
Betwixt them lawns and level downs, and flocks
Grazing the tender herb, were interposed,
Or palmy hillock; or the flowery lap
Of some irriguous valley spread her store,
Flowers of all hue, and without thorn, the rose :
Another side, umbrageous grots and caves
Of cool recess, o'er which the mantling vine
Lays forth her purple grapes, and gently creeps
Luxuriant; meanwhile murmuring waters fall
Down the slope hills, dispersed, or in a lake,
That to the fringèd bank with myrtle crowned
Her crystal mirror holds, unite their streams.
The birds their choir apply; airs, vernal airs,
Breathing the smell of field and grove, attune
The trembling leaves, while universal Pan,
Knit with the Graces and the Hours in dance,
Led on the eternal Spring.

EVE'S RECOLLECTIONS.

THAT day I oft remember, when from sleep
I first awaked, and found myself reposed
Under a shade on flowers, much wondering where
And what I was, whence thither brought, and how.
Not distant far from thence, a murmuring sound
Of waters issued from a cave, and spread
Into a liquid plain, then stood unmoved
Pure as the expanse of heaven. I thither went
With unexperienced thought, and laid me down
On the green bank, to look into the clear
Smooth lake, that to me seem'd another sky.
As I bent down to look, just opposite
A shape within the watery gleam appear'd,
Bending to look on me: I started back,
It started back; but pleased I soon return'd,
Pleased it return'd as soon with answering looks
Of sympathy and love.

EVE TO ADAM.

With thee conversing I forget all time ;
All seasons, and their change, all please alike.
Sweet is the breath of Morn, her rising sweet,
With charm of earliest birds; pleasant the Sun,
When first on this delightful land he spreads
His orient beams on herb, tree, fruit, and flower,
Glistering with dew : fragrant the fertile Earth
After soft showers; and sweet the coming on
Of grateful Evening mild; then silent Night,
With this her solemn bird, and this fair Moon,
And these the gems of Heaven, her starry train.
But neither breath of Morn, when she ascends
With charm of earliest birds; nor rising Sun
On this delightful land; nor herb, fruit, flower,
Glistering with dew; nor fragrance after showers,
Nor grateful Evening mild; nor silent Night,
With this her solemn bird; nor walk by Moon
Or glittering star-light, without thee, is sweet.

"ADAM, WHERE ART THOU?"

Adam, where art thou? monarch, where?
 It is thy Maker calls:
What means that look of wild despair,
 What anguish now enthralls?
Why in the wood's embowering shade,
 Dost thou attempt to hide,
From Him Whose hand thy kingdom made,
 And all thy wants supplied?
Go hide again, thou fallen one,
 The crown has left thy brow ;
The robe of purity is gone,
 And thou art naked now.

Adam, where art thou ? monarch, where ?
 Assert thy high command ?
Call forth the tiger from his lair,
 To lick thy kingly hand ;
Control the air, control the earth,
 Control the foaming sea ;
They own no more thy heavenly birth,

Or heaven-stamp'd royalty.
The brutes no longer will caress
  But share with thee thy reign;
For the sceptre of thy righteousness,
  Thy hands have snapped in twain.

Adam, where art thou? monarch, where?
  Thou wondrous thing of clay;
Ah! let the earthworm now declare,
  Who claims thee as his prey;
Thy mother, oh thou mighty one,
  For thee re-opes her womb;
Thou to the narrow house art gone,
  Thy kingdom is thy tomb;
The truth from Godhead's lips that came,
  There in thy darkness learn;
Of dust was formed thy beauteous frame,
  And shall to dust return.

Adam, where art thou? where! ah where?
  Behold him raised above,
An everlasting life to share,
  In the bright world of love.
The hand he once 'gainst heaven could raise,
  Another sceptre holds;
His brows where new-born glories blaze,
  Another crown enfolds.
Another robe's flung over him,
  More fair than was his own;
And with the fire-tongued seraphim,
  He dwells before the throne.

But whence could such a change proceed?
  What power could raise him there?
So late by God's own voice decreed
  Transgression's curse to bear.
Hark! hark! he tells—a harp well strung
  His grateful arms embrace;
Salvation is his deathless song,
  And grace, abounding grace;
And sounds through all the upper sky
  A strain with wonders rife,
That Life hath given itself to die,
  And bring death back to life.

ADAM AND EVE LEAVING PARADISE.

So spake our Mother Eve ; and Adam heard
Well-pleased, but answered not : for now too nigh
The Archangel stood ; and from the other hill
To their fixed station, all in bright array,
The Cherubim descended; on the ground
Gliding meteorous, as evening mist
Risen from a river o'er the marish glides,
And gathers ground, fast at the labourer's heel
Homeward returning. High in front advanced
The brandished sword of God before them blazed,
Fierce as a comet ; which, with torrid heat
And vapours as the Lybian air adust,
Began to parch that temperate clime; whereat
In either hand the hast'ning Angel caught
Our lingering parents ; and to th'eastern gate
Led them direct and down the cliff as fast
To the subjected plain : then disappeared.
They, looking back, all the eastern side beheld
Of Paradise; so late their happy seat!
Waved over by that flaming brand ; the gate
With dreadful faces thronged and fiery arms.
Some natural tears they dropped, but wiped them soon ;
The world was all before them, where to choose
Their place of rest, and Providence their guide.
They, hand in hand, with wandering steps and slow,
Through Eden took their solitary way.

EVE'S FIRST BORN.

For the first time, a lovely scene
   Earth saw, and smiled—
A gentle form with pallid mien,
   Bending o'er a new-born child.
The pang, the anguish, and the woe
   That speech hath never told,
Fled, as the sun with noontide glow
   Dissolves the snow-wreath cold,
Leaving the bliss that none but mothers know,
   While he, the partner of her heaven-taught joy,
Knelt in adoring praise beside the beauteous boy.

She, first of all our mortal race,
  Learned the ecstacy to trace
The expanding form of infant grace,
From her own life-spring fed ;
  To mark each radiant hour,
Heaven's sculpture still more perfect growing,
  More full of power ;
The little foot's elastic tread,
The rounded cheek, like rose-bud glowing,
The fringèd eye with gladness flowing
  As the pure blue fountains roll ;
And then those lisping sounds to hear,
Unfolding to her thrilling ear
  The strange, mysterious, never-dying soul,
And with delight intense
To watch the angel-smile of sleeping innocence.

No more she mourned lost Eden's joy,
  Or wept her cherished flowers,
  In their primeval bowers,
By wrecking tempest riven ;
  The thorn and thistle of the exile's lot
  She heeded not,
So all absorbing was her sweet employ
To rear the incipient man, the gift her God had given.

"CAIN, WHERE IS THY BROTHER ABEL?"

Where is thy brother Abel ?
  Thou murderer, answer, where ?
He talked with thee on yonder plain,
  Beside the altar there;
Sweet peace was in his eye serene,
  And his heart was fill'd with love;
As he pointed thy unbended soul
  To Him who reigns above.

Where is thy brother Abel ?
  Thou fratricide, ah ! where ?
Thy heart, in childhood's earlier hours,
  His joy or grief could share ;
Ye danced beneath the same green tree ;
  In the same bower ye played;
And oft have wandered hand in hand,
  Beneath the grove's deep shade.

'Where is thy brother Abel?
  Unfeeling one, ah! where?
Lock'd in each other's fond embrace,
  Ye once could know no care;
Nor the silence nor the gloom of night
  Could wake an anxious fear,
While in each other's arms ye lay,
  Or felt each other near.

Where is thy brother Abel?
  Ungrateful one, ah! where?
His lips dwelt long upon thy name
  As he breathed his morning prayer;
He begged that Heaven would fix thy faith,
  On Him that is to come,
To take away the curse of sin,
  And bring God's outcasts home.

'Where is thy brother Abel?
  Thy red hands answer where,
No light is in his sunken eye,
  No smiles his cold cheeks bear;
His lips are closed; his tongue is sealed;
  His locks are wet with gore;
The cooling breeze revives him not,
  'Twill wake him now no more.

His blood has raised its voice to heaven,
  And calls for vengeance loud;
Yet mercy still, with smiling face,
  Looks o'er the thunder cloud;
But a fugitive and a vagabond,
  Thou now on earth shalt be,
Though the latest breath that passed his lips
  Was spent in prayer for thee.

CAIN ON THE SEA-SHORE.

Woe is me! oh where, oh where
Doth my spirit drive me? where?
These wild torrents roll to me
Abel's blood!—It is the sea!

E'en to earth's remotest verge
Vengeance doth me onward urge!

Where no tongue did e'er complain,
Abel's blood has banished Cain!

Woe is me! My brother's blood
Thunders in the roaring flood!
In the rocky beach's sound!
In the cavern's loud rebound!

As the waves beat round the rock,
So my spirit feels the shock
Of grief and rage, anguished mood,
Dread of Heaven, Abel's blood!

Open, waves, your surging tide!
For the earth, when Abel died,
Drank the blood of him I slew,
Heard the curse of vengeance too!

Open, waves, your surging tide!
And disclose your bed all wide!
Ah 'tis vain! revenge has might
In the realm of ancient night!

In the darkest, deepest deep,
Abel's shade would near me keep —
Near me, though I took my flight
To the highest mountain's height.

Should this frame dissolve away,
Of the whirlpool-storm the prey,
Yet, oh yet, would Cain still dread
Heaven's anger on his head!

Knowing now no end, no age,
My tormented spirit's rage
(Time's remotest bound'ries past)
Through unceasing years will last.

Vengeance on my head I drew,
Th' instant I my brother slew!
Woe is me! oh woe is me!
Dread of Heaven follows me!

ENOCH WALKED WITH GOD.

He walked with God, in holy joy,
    While yet his days were few;
The deep glad spirit of the boy
    To love and reverence grew.
Whether, each nightly star to count
    The ancient hills he trod,
Or sought the flowers by stream and fount—
    Alike he walked with God.

The graver noon of manhood came,
    The time of cares and fears;
One voice was in his heart—the same
    It heard through childhood's years.
Amid fair tents, and flocks and swains,
    O'er his green pasture sod,
A shepherd king on eastern plains,
    The patriarch walked with God.

And calmly, brightly, that pure life
    Melted from earth away;
No cloud it knew, no parting strife,
    No sorrowful decay;
He bow'd him not, like all beside,
    Unto the spoiler's rod,
But join'd at once the glorified
    Where angels walk with God!

So let us walk!—the night must come
    To us that comes to all;
We through the darkness must go home,
    Hearing the tempest's call.
Closed is the path for evermore
    Which without death he trod;
Not so that way wherein of yore
    His footsteps walk'd with God.

THE DELUGE.

Morn came, but the broad light, which hung so long
In heaven, forsook the showering firmament,
The clouds went floating on their fatal way.
Rivers had grown to seas: the great sea swollen,
Too mighty for its bounds, broke on the land,
Roaring and rushing, and each flat and plain
Devoured. Upon the mountains now were seen
Gaunt men and women hungering with their babes
Eyeing each other, or, with marble looks,
Measuring the space beneath, swift lessening.
At times a swimmer from a distant rock
Less high, came struggling with the waves, but sank
Back from the slippery soil. Pale mothers then
Wept without hope, and agèd heads struck cold
By agues, trembling like autumnal leaves;
And infants mourned, and young boys shrieked with fear.
Stout men grew white with famine. Beautiful girls,
Whom once the day languished to look on, lay
On the wet earth, and rung their drenching hair;
And fathers saw them there dying, and stole
Their scanty fare, and, while they perished, thrived.
Then terror died, and grief, and proud despair,
Rage, and remorse, infinite agony,
Love in its thousand shapes, weak and sublime,
Birth-strangled; and strong passion perished.
The young, the old, weak, wise, the bad, the good,
Fell on their faces, struck,—whilst over them
Washed the wild waters, in their clamorous march.
Still fell the flooding rains. Great Ossa stood
Lone, like a peering Alp, when vapours shroud
Its sides unshaken in the restless waves:
But from the weltering deeps Pelion arose,
And shook his piny forehead at the clouds,
Moaning; and crowned Olympus all his snows
Lost from his hundred heads, and shrank aghast.
Day, eve, night, morning, came and passed away,
No sun was known to rise and none to set:
'Stead of its glorious beams a sickly light
Paled the broad cast what time the day is born;
At others a thick mass, vapours and black
In form like solid marble, roofed the sky,
Yet gave no shelter. Still the ravenous wolf
Howled; the wild foxes, and the household dog
Grown wild, upon the mountains fought and fed
Each on the other. The great eagle still
In his home brooded, inaccessible;

* Or, when the gloomy morning seemed to break,
Floated in silence on the shoreless seas.
Still the quick snake unclasped its glittering eyes,
Or shivering hung about the roots of pines;
And still all round the vultures flew and watched
The tumbling waters thick with bird and beast;
Or, dashing in the midst their ravenous beaks,
Plundered the rolling billows of their dead.
Beneath the headlong torrents, towns and towers
Fell down; temples all stone, and brazen shrines,
And piles of marble, Palace and Pyramid
(Kings' homes or towering graves) in a breath were swept
Crumbling away. Masses of ground, and trees
Uptorn and floating, hollow rocks brute-crammed,
Vast herds, and bleating flocks, reptiles, and beasts
Bellowing, and vainly with the choking waves
Struggling, were hurried out,—but none returned:
All on the altar of the giant sea
Offered, like twice ten thousand hecatombs.
Still fell the flooding rains, still the earth shrank!
And ruin held his strait terrific way.
Fierce lightnings burnt the sky, and the loud thunder
(Breast of fiery air) howled from his cloud,
Exalting toward the storm eclipsèd moon.
Below, the ocean rose boiling and black
And flung its monstrous billows far and wide,
Crumbling the mountain joints and summit hills:
Then its dark throat is bared, and rocky tusks,
Where with enormous waves on their broad backs
The demons of the deep were raging loud:
And the sea lion and the whale were swung,
Like atoms round and round. Mankind was dead;
And birds whose active wings once cut the air,
The beasts that cut the water, all were dead:
And every reptile of the woods had died,
Which crawled or stung, and every curling worm:
The untamed tiger in his den, the mole
In his dark home—were choked; the darting ounce,
An the blind adder, and the stork fell down
Dead;—and the stifled mammoth, a vast bulk,
Was washed far out amongst the populous foam.
And there the serpent, which, few hours ago,
Could crack the panther in his scaly folds,
Lay lifeless, like a weed, beside his prey.
And now, all o'er the deep, corses were strewn,
Wide floating millions, like the rubbish flung
Forth when a plague prevails, the rest down sucked,
Sank buried in the world-destroying seas.

SUBSIDING OF THE WATERS OF THE DELUGE.

HE looked and saw the ark hull on the flood,
Which now abated ; for the clouds were fled,
Driven by a keen north wind, that blowing dry,
Wrinkled the face of Deluge, as decayed :
And the clear Sun on his wide watery glass
Glazed hot, and of the fresh wave largely drew,
As after thirst ; which made their flowing shrink
From standing lake to tripping ebb, that stole
With soft foot towards the Deep ; who now had stopt
His sluices, as the Heaven his windows shut.
The ark no more now floats, but seems on ground,
Fast on the top of some high mountain fixed.
And now the tops of hills, as rocks, appear ;
With clamour thence the rapid currents drive,
Towards the retreating sea, their furious tide.
Forthwith from out the ark a raven flies,
And after him the surer messenger,
A dove, sent forth once and again to spy
Green tree or ground, whereon his foot may light :
The second time returning, in his bill
An olive leaf he brings, pacific sign :
Anon, dry ground appears, and from his ark
The ancient Sire descends, with all his train,
Then with uplifted hands, and eyes devout,
Grateful to Heaven, over his head beholds
A dewy cloud, and in the cloud a bow
Conspicuous with three listed colours gay,
Betokening peace from God, and covenant new.

TO THE RAINBOW.

TRIUMPHAL arch, that fill'st the sky
   When storms prepare to part,
I ask not proud Philosophy
   To teach me what thou art.

Still seem, as to my childhood's sight,
   A mid-way station given,

For happy spirits to alight
   Betwixt the earth and heaven.

Can all, that optics teach, unfold
   Thy form to please me so,
As when I dreamt of gems and gold
   Hid in thy radiant bow?

When Science from Creation's face
   Enchantment's veil withdraws,
What lovely visions yield their place
   To cold material laws!

And yet, fair bow, no fabling dreams,
   But words of the Most High,
Have told why first thy robe of beams
   Was woven in the sky.

When o'er the green undeluged earth
   Heaven's covenant thou didst shine,
How came the world's grey fathers forth,
   To watch thy sacred sign.

And when its yellow lustre smiled,
   O'er mountains yet untrod,
Each mother held aloft her child,
   To bless the bow of God.

Methinks, thy jubilee to keep,
   The first-made anthem rang
On earth, delivered from the deep,
   And the first poet sang.

Nor ever shall the Muse's eye,
   Unraptured greet thy beam;
Theme of primeval prophecy,
   Be still the poet's theme!

The earth to thee her incense yields,
   The lark thy welcome sings,
When glittering in the freshened fields,
   The snowy mushroom springs.

How glorious is thy girdle cast
   O'er mountain, tower, and town.
Or mirrored in the ocean vast,
   A thousand fathoms down!

As fresh in yon horizon dark,
   As young thy beauties seem,

As when the eagle from the ark
　　First sported in thy beam.

For, faithful to its sacred page,
　　Heaven still rebuilds thy span,
Nor lets the type grow pale with age,
　　That first spoke peace to man.

THE DESTRUCTION OF SODOM.

The wind blows chill across those gloomy waves;
　　Oh! how unlike the green and dancing main!
The surge is foul, as if it rolled o'er graves:
　　Stranger, here lie the cities of the plain.

Yes, on that plain, by wild waves covered now,
　　Rose palace once and sparkling pinnacle;
On pomp and spectacle beamed morning's glow,
　　On pomp and festival the twilight fell.

Lovely and splendid all,—but Sodom's soul
　　Was stained with blood, and pride, and perjury;
Long warned, long spared, till her whole heart was foul,
　　And fiery vengeance on its clouds came nigh.

And still she mocked, and danced, and, taunting, spoke
　　Her sportive blasphemies against the Throne:
It came! The thunder on her slumber broke:
　　God spake the word of wrath!—Her dream was done.

Yet, in her final night, amid her stood
　　Immortal messengers, and pausing Heaven
Pleaded with man; but she was quite imbued,
　　Her last hour waned, she scorned to be forgiven!

'Twas done! down poured at once the sulphurous shower,
　　Down stooped, in flame, the heaven's red canopy,
Oh! for the arm of God, in that fierce hour!
　　'Twas vain; nor help of God or man was nigh.

They rush, they bound, they howl, the men of sin;
　　Still stooped the cloud, still burst the thicker blaze;
The earthquake heaved! Then sank the hideous din:
　　Yon wave of darkness o'er their ashes strays.

ABRAHAM'S SACRIFICE.

The noontide sun streamed brightly down
On Moriah's mountain crest,
The golden blaze of his vivid rays
Tinged sacred Jordan's breast;
Whilst towering palms and flowerets sweet,
Drooped low 'neath Syria's burning heat.

In the sunny glare of the sultry air,
Toiled up the mountain side,
The Patriarch sage in stately age,
And a youth in health's gay pride,
Bearing in eyes and in features fair,
The stamp of his mother's beauty rare.

She had not known when one rosy dawn
Ere they'd started on their way,
She had smoothed with care, his clustering hair,
And knelt with him to pray,
That his father's hand and will alike,
Were nerved at his young heart to strike.

The Heavenly Power that with such dower
Of love fills a mother's heart,
Ardent and pure, that can all endure,
Of her life itself a part,
Knew too well that love beyond all price,
To ask of her such a sacrifice.

Though the noble boy with laughing joy
Had borne on the mountain road,
Th' holocaust wood, which in mournful mood,
His sire had helped to load,
Type of Him who dragged up Calvary,
The cross on which He was to die.

The hot breath of noon began, ah! soon,
On his youthful frame to tell,
On the ivory brow, flushed, wearied, now,
It laid its burning spell.
And listless—heavy—he journeyed on,
The smiles from his lips and bright eyes gone.

Once did he say, on their toilsome way,
"Father, no victim is near,"
But with heavy sigh and tear dimmed eye,
In accents sad though clear,

Abraham answered: " The Lord our Guide;.
A fitting holocaust will provide."

The altar made and the fuel laid,
Lo ! the victim stretched thereon
Is Abraham's son, his only one,
Who at morning's blushing dawn,
Had started with smiles that care defied,
To travel on at his father's side.

With grief-struck brow, the Patriarch now,
Bares the sharp and glittering knife,
On that mournful pyre, oh hapless Sire !
Must he take his darling's life;
Will fails not, though his eyes are dim,
God gave his Boy—he belongs to Him.

With anguish riven, he casts towards heaven,
One look, imploring wild,
That doth mutely pray for strength, to slay
His own, aye ! his only child ;
When forth on the air swells a glad command,
And an angel stays his trembling hand.

The offering done—father and son
Come down Mount Moriah's steep,
Joy gleaming now on Abraham's brow,
In his heart thanksgiving deep ;
Whilst from His far and resplendent Throne,
With love, Heaven's King on both looks down.

HAGAR AND ISHMAEL.

" Ah me ! My son, my son !
Pitiless light pours down the burning sky,
And water there is none."

" My mother ! is it night ? "
" Th' accursèd sun hath blinded his sweet eyes,
Those living wells of light.

" Night in the midst of noon,—
O would that it were death, that he might wake
No more out of his swoon.

"But he will waken wild
With thirst, and rave, and water there is none—
 Oh, God! my child! my child!

"Would I my soul could pour
Out like a well-spring in this scorching waste,
 That he might thirst no more.

"Would he my life might drain,
As once my breast, I'd hold it to his lips,
 That he might live again.

"I cannot see him die—
O God, how canst thou see it up in Heaven,
 Nor help, if Thou art nigh?

"Wilt Thou cast off for aye,
Like Abram? Hast Thou not enough for all?
 That all may hope and pray.

"Yea, if Thou art the Lord,
Uncovenanted though thy mercy be,
 Wilt thou not help afford?"

She ceased! A stony look
Uplifting to the burning sky once more,
 The fainting lad she took,

And lifted him with care
Into the shadow of a rock, and strode
 Away in her despair.

She will not see him die;
But hears her heart throb in the voiceless waste,
 While listening for his cry.

And listening thus there breaks
A mystic murmur on her straining ear—
 As from a dream she wakes.

A mist before her eyes
Of angel wings departing—a white cloud
 That lessens up the skies.

And at her feet she knows,
From the soft gush among the sinking sand,
 The living water flows.

ABRAHAM AT MACHPELAH.

    DENSELY wrapped in shades
Olive and terebinth, its vaulted door
Flecked with the untrained vine and matted grass,
Behold Machpelah's cave.
    Hark ! hear we not
A voice of weeping ? Lo, yon agèd man
Bendeth beside his dead. Wave after wave
Of memory rises, till his lonely heart
Sees all its treasures floating on the flood
Like rootless weeds.
    The earliest dawn of love
Is present with him, and a form of grace
Whose beauty held him ever in its thrall :
And then the morn of marriage, gorgeous robes
And dulcet music and the rites that bless
The Eastern bride. Full many a glowing scene
Made happy by her tenderness, returns
To mock his solitude.
    Again their home
Gleams through the oaks of Mamre. There he sat
Rendering due rites of hospitality
To guests who bore the folded wing of Heaven
Beneath their vestments. And her smile was there
Among the angels.
    When her clustering curls
Wore Time's chill hoar frost, with what glad surprise
What holy triumphs of exulting faith
He saw, fresh blooming in her withered arms,
A fair young babe, the heir of all his wealth,
For ever blending with that speechless joy
Which thrilled his soul when first a father's name
Fell on his ear, is that pale, placid brow
O'er which he weeps.
    Yet had he seen it wear
Another semblance, tinged with hues of thought
Perchance, unlovely in that trial hour
When to sad Hagar's mute reproachful eyes
He answered nought, but on her shoulder bound
The cruse of water and the loaf, and sent
Her and her son unfriended wanderers forth
Into the wilderness.
    Say, who can mourn
Over the smitten idol, by long years
Cemented with his being, yet perceive
No dark remembrance that he fain would blot,
Troubling the tear ? If there were no kind deed

Omitted, no sweet healing word of love
Expected yet unspoken ; no sharp tone,
That jarred discordant on the quivering nerve,
For which the weeper fain would rend the tomb
To cry, " Forgive ! " oh ! let him kneel and praise
God, amid all his grief.
        We may not say
If aught of penitence was in the pang
That rung his laboring breast, while o'er the dust
Of Sarah, at Machpelah's watery tomb,
The proud and princely Abraham bowed him down
A mourning stranger, 'mid the sons of Heth.

THE REPENTANCE OF ESAU.

The eastern moon rose broad and red
    Against the Western Sun ;
The fring'd palm higher rais'd its head,
    The day's fierce reign was done.

The Patriarch's tent stood cool and white
    And dark the shade it threw,
While dim and far and lost in night
    The sands drank in the dew.

A vaguely solemn, silent scene,
    Round Sheba's Valley slept ;
When from the tent's white folds between,
    A voice of one who wept.

The cry throughout the valley past
    Contrition and despair,
" One Blessing Father, all thou hast !
    None left for me ! thine heir ! "

The palm trees wav'd, the moon rose high.
    The misty desert spread,
How could be check'd by mortals cry
    Nature's majestic tread ?

The night absorb'd the transient sound,
    No rock gave back the sigh,
All unresponsive was around,
    To frail man's agony.

Oh nature! cruel to thy child!
  How many a bitter pain,
Since that lone cry upon the wild
  Hath sought thy breast in vain!

One blessing only, Mother Earth!
  Can no hot tears efface?
Is all Remorse but nothing worth
  Past errors to retrace?

No! Nature's Laws cannot reverse
  For man's inconstant mind,
And one must reap the whirlwind curse
  If one have sown the wind.

One blessing and forever gone!
  Oh dreary coming years!
Inexorable world roll on!
  Thou canst not stay for tears!

Yet far beyond earth's utmost zone
  The King of Kings most high,
And all the Angels round His Throne
  Catch each remorseful sigh;

There the Repentant need not stand
  In sorrow all in vain,
That in his Heavenly Father's Hand
  No blessings still remain.

For there are "many Mansions" fair
  And Joys beyond our thought,
Such as ne'er fill'd the raptur'd ear
  Nor trainèd eye hath caught.

Then "lift the drooping hands" once more
  And "bend the feeble knees"
To Him who only can restore,
  And ev'ry grief appease.

JACOB'S DREAM.

The sun was sinking on the mountain zone
That guard thy vales of beauty, Palestine!
And lovely from the desert rose the moon
Yet lingering on the horizon's purple line,

Like a pure spirit o'er its earthly shrine.
Up Padan-aram's height abrupt and bare
A pilgrim toil'd, and oft on day's decline
Look'd pale, then paused for eve's delicious air ;
The summit gain'd, he knelt and breathed his evening prayer.

He spread his cloak and slumber'd—darkness fell
Upon the twilight hills ; a sudden sound
Of silver trumpets o'er him seem'd to swell ;
Clouds heavy with the tempest gather'd round ;
Yet was the whirlwind in its caverns bound :
Still deeper roll'd the darkness from on high,
Gigantic volume upon volume wound,
Above, a pillar shooting to the sky,
Below, a mighty sea, that spread incessantly.

Voices are heard—a choir of golden strings,
Low winds, whose breath is loaded with the rose,
Then chariot-wheels—the nearer rush of wings ;
Pale lightning round the dark pavilion glows,
It thunders—the resplendent gates unclose :
Far as the eye can glance, on height o'er height,
Rise fiery waving wings, and star-crown'd brows,
Millions on millions, brighter and more bright,
Till all is lost in one supreme, unmingled light.

But, two beside the sleeping pilgrim stand,
Like cherub-kings, with lifted, mighty plume,
Fix'd, sun-bright eyes, and looks of high command ;
They tell the patriarch of his glorious doom ;
Father of countless myriads that shall come,
Sweeping the land like billows of the sea,
Bright as the stars of heaven from twilight's gloom,
Till He is given whom angels long to see,
And Israel's splendid line is crown'd with Deity.

JACOB WRESTLING WITH THE ANGEL.

I.

Come, O Thou traveller unknown,
Whom still I hold, but cannot see ;
My company before is gone,
And I am left alone with Thee ;
With Thee all night I mean to stay,
And wrestle till the break of day.

I need not tell Thee who I am;
My misery and sin declare :
Thyself hast called me by my name ;
Look on Thy hands, and read it there :
But who, I ask Thee, who art Thou ?
Tell me Thy name, and tell me now.

In vain Thou strugglest to get free,
I never will unloose my hold ;
Art Thou the Man that died for me ?
The secret of Thy love unfold :
Wrestling, I will not let Thee go,
Till I Thy name, Thy nature know.

Wilt Thou not yet to me reveal
Thy new, unutterable name ?
Tell me, I still beseech Thee, tell ?
To know it now, resolved I am :
Wrestling, I will not let Thee go,
Till I Thy name, Thy nature know.

What though my shrinking flesh complain,
And murmur to contend so long ?
I rise superior to my pain :
When I am weak, then I am strong,
And when my all of strength shall fail,
I shall with the GOD-MAN prevail.

II.

YIELD to me now, for I am weak,
But confident in self-despair,
Speak to my heart, in blessings speak;
Be conquer'd by my instant prayer :
Speak, or Thou never hence shalt move,
And tell me if Thy name be Love.

'Tis Love !—'tis Love ! Thou diedst for me;
I hear Thy whisper in my heart:
The morning breaks, the shadows flee;
Pure, Universal Love, Thou art:
To me, to all, Thy bowels move;
Thy nature and Thy name is Love.

My prayer hath power with God; the grace
Unspeakable I now receive;
Through faith I see Thee face to face;
I see Thee face to face, and live;
In vain I have not wept and strove;
Thy nature and Thy name is Love.

I know Thee, Saviour, who Thou art,
Jesus, the feeble sinner's Friend:
Nor wilt Thou with the night depart,
But stay and love me to the end:
Thy mercies never shall remove;
Thy nature and Thy name is Love.

The Sun of Righteousness on me
Hath risen, with healing on His wings;
Wither'd my nature's strength; from Thee
My soul its life and succor brings;
My help is all laid up above;
Thy nature and Thy name is Love.

Contented now upon my thigh
I halt, till life's short journey end;
All helplessness, all weakness, I
On Thee alone for strength depend;
Nor have I power from Thee to move:
Thy nature and Thy name is Love.

Lame as I am, I take the prey;
Hell, earth, and sin, with ease o'ercome;
I leap for joy, pursue my way,
And, as a bounding hart, fly home;
Through all eternity, to prove
Thy nature and Thy name is Love.

THE BURIAL OF JACOB.

It is a solemn cavalcade, and slow,
  That comes from Egypt; never had the land,
Save when a Pharaoh died, such pomp of woe
  Beheld; never was bier by such a band
Of princely mourners followed, and the grand
Gloom of that strange funereal armament
Saddened the wondering cities as it went.

In Goshen he had died, that region fair
  Which stretches east from Nilus to the wave
Of the great Gulf; and since he could not bear
  To lay his ashes in an alien grave,
  He charged his sons to bear him to the cave
Where slumbered all his kin, that from life's cares
And weariness his dust might rest with theirs.

For seventy days through Egypt ran the cry
    Of woe, for Joseph wept: and now there came
Along with him the rank and chivalry
    Of Pharaoh's court, — the flower of Egypt's fame;
    High captains, chief estates, and lords of name,
The prince, the priest, the warrior, and the sage,
Made haste to join in that sad pilgrimage.

The hoary elders in their robes of state
    Were there, and sceptred judges; and the sight
Of their pavilions pitched without the gate
    Was pleasant; chariots with their trappings bright
    Stood round, — till all were met, and every rite
Was paid; — then at a signal the array
Moved with a heavy spendour on its way.

Its very gloom was gorgeous; and the sound
    Of brazen chariots, and the measured feet
Of stately pacing steeds upon the ground,
    Seemed, by its dead and dull monotonous beat,
    A burden to that march of sorrow meet;
With music Pharaoh's minstrels would have come
Had Joseph wished, — 'twas better they were dumb.

They pass by many a town then famed or feared,
    But quite forgotten now; and over ground
Then waste, on which in after time were reared
    Cities whose names were of familiar sound
    For centuries, — Bubastus, and renowned
Pelusium, whose glories in decay
Gorged the lean desert with a splendid prey.

The fiery sons of Ishmael, as they scour
    The stony glens of Paran with their hordes,
Watch their array afar, but dread their power;
    Here first against mankind they drew their swords
    In open warfare; as the native lords
Of the wild region held their free career,
And fenced the desert with the Arab spear.

But unmolested now the mourners pass,
    Till distant trees, like signs of land, appear,
And pleasantly they feel the yielding grass
    Beneath their feet, and in the morning clear
    They see with joy the hills of Canaan near;
The camels scent the freshness of the wells,
Far hidden in the depth of leafy dells.

At length they reach a valley opening fair
    With harvest field and homestead in the sweep
Of olive-sprinkled hills, where they prepare

The solemn closing obsequies to keep;
For an appointed time they rest, and weep
With ceaseless lamentation, and the land
Rings with a grief it cannot understand.

The rites thus duly paid, they onward went
  Across the eastern hills, and rested not
Till, slowly winding up the last ascent,
  They see the walls of Hebron, and the spot
To him they bore so dear and unforgot,
Where the dark cypress and the sycamore
Weave their deep shadows round the rock-hewn door.

Now Jacob rests where all his kindred are,—
  The exile from the land in which of old
His fathers lived and died, he comes from far
  To mix his ashes with their mortal mould.
There where he stood with Esau, in the cold
Dim passage of the vault, with holy trust
His sons lay down the venerable dust.

They laid him close by Leah, where she sleeps
  Far from her Syrian home, and never knows
That Reuben kneels beside her feet and weeps,
  Nor glance of kindly recognition throws
Upon her stately sons from that repose;
His Rachel rests far-sundered from his side,
Upon the way to Bethlehem, where she died.

Sleep on, O weary saint! thy bed is bless'd;
  Thou, with the pilgrim-staff of faith, hast pass'd
Another Jordan into endless rest:
  Well may they sleep who can serenely cast
  A look behind, while darkness closes fast
Upon their path, and breathe thy parting word,—
"For Thy salvation I have waited, Lord!"

THE FINDING OF MOSES.

Slow glides the Nile; amid the margin flags,
Closed in a bulrush ark, the babe is left,—
Left by a mother's hand. His sister waits
Far off; and pale, 'tween hope and fear, beholds
The royal maid surrounded by her train,
Approach the river bank,—approach the spot

Where sleeps the innocent: she sees them stoop
With meeting plumes; the rushy lid is ope'd
And wakes the infant smiling in his tears,
As when along a little mountain lake,
The summer south wind breathes, with gentle sigh,
And parts the reeds, unveiling as they bend,
A water-lily floating on the wave.

JOCHEBED'S SOLILOQUY.

" I've almost reach'd the place—with cautious steps
" I must approach the spot where he is laid,
" Lest from the royal gardens any see me.
" Poor babe! ere this, the pressing calls of hunger
" Have broke thy short repose; the chilling waves,
" Ere this, have drench'd thy little shivering limbs.
" What must my babe have suffered—No one sees me,
" But soft, does no one listen! Ah! how hard,
" How very hard for fondness to be prudent!
" Now is the moment to embrace and feed him.
" Where's Miriam, she has left her little charge,
" Perhaps through fear; perhaps she was detected.
" How wild is thought? how terrible is conjecture!
" A mother's fondness frames a thousand fears,
" With thrilling nerve feels every real ill,
" And shapes imagined miseries into being.
" Ah me! Where is he? soul-distracting sight!
" He is not there—he's lost, he's gone, he's drown'd!
" Toss'd by each beating surge my infant floats.
" Cold, cold, and watery is thy grave, my child!
" Oh no—I see the ark—Transporting sight!
" I have it here. Alas, the ark is empty!
" The casket's left, the precious gem is gone!
" You spared him, pitying spirits of the deep
" But vain your mercy; some insatiate beast,
" Cruel as Pharaoh, took the life you spared—
" And I shall never, never see my boy!"

THE SEVENTH PLAGUE OF EGYPT.

'Twas morn—the rising splendor rolled
On marble towers and roofs of gold;
Hall, court and gallery, below,
Were crowded with a living flow;
Egyptian, Arab, Nubian, there,—
The bearers of the bow and spear,
The hoary priest, the Chaldee sage,
The slave, the gemm'd and glittering page—
Helm, turban and tiara, shone
A dazzling ring round Pharaoh's throne.

There came a man—the human tide
Shrunk backward from his stately stride :
His cheek with storm and tide was tanned ;
A shepherd's staff was in is hand ;
A shudder of instinctive fear
Told the dark king what step was near;
On through the host the stranger came,
It parted round his form like flame.

He stooped not at the foot-stool stone,
He clasped not sandal, kissed not throne ;
Erect he stood amid the ring.
His only words—" Be just, O King !"
On Pharaoh's cheek the blood flushed high,
A fire was in his sullen eye;
Yet on the chief of Israel
No arrow of his thousands fell ;
All mute and moveless as the grave
Stood chilled the satrap and the slave.

" Thou'rt come," at length the monarch spoke,
Haughty and high the words outbroke :
" Is Israel weary of its lair,
The forehead peeled, the shoulder bare ?
Take back the answer to your band :
Go, reap the wind ! go, plough the sand.
Go, vilest of the living vile,
To build the never ending pile,
Till, darkest of the nameless dead,
The vulture on their flesh is fed !
What better asks the howling slave
Than the base life our bounty gave ?"

Shouted in pride the turban'd peers
Unclasp'd to heaven the golden spears.

" King ! thou and thine are doomed !—Behold ! "
The prophet spoke—the thunder rolled !
Along the pathway of the sun
Sailed vapory mountains, wild and dun.
" Yet there is time," the prophet said :
He raised his staff—the storm was stayed :
" King ! be the word of freedom given ;
What art thou, man, to war with Heaven ?"

There came no word—the thunder broke !
Like a huge city's final smoke ;—
Thick, lurid, stifling, mixed with flame,
Through court and hall the vapours came.
Loose as the stubble in the field,
Wide flew the men of spear and shield ;
Scattered like foam along the wave,
Flew the proud pageant, prince and slave :
Or, in the chains of terror bound,
Lay, corpse-like, on the smouldering ground.
" Speak, King ! — the wrath is but begun !—
Still dumb ?—then, Heaven, thy will be done !"

Echoed from earth a hollow roar
Like ocean on the midnight shore !
A sheet of lightning o'er them wheeled,
The solid ground beneath them reeled ;
In dusk sank roof and battlement ;.
Like webs the giant walls were rent ;
Red, broad, before his startled gaze
The monarch saw his Egypt blaze.
Still swelled the plague—the flame grew pale
Burst from the clouds the charge of hail
With arrowy keenness, iron weight,
Down poured the ministers of fate ;
Till man and cattle, crushed, congealed,
Covered with death the boundless field.

Still swelled the plague—uprose the blast,
The avenger fit to be the last :
On ocean, river, forest, vale,
Thunder'd at once the mighty gale.
Before the whirlwind flew the tree,
Beneath the whirlwind roar'd the sea,
A thousand ships were on the wave : —
Where are they ? —ask that foaming grave
Down go the hope, the pride of years,
Down go the myriad mariners ;
The riches of earth's richest zone
Gone ! like a flash of lightning, gone !

And, lo ! that first fierce triumph o'er,
Swells ocean on the shrinking shore ;
Still onward, onward, dark and wide,
Engulfs the land the furious tide.
Then bowed thy spirit, stubborn king,
Thou serpent reft of fang and sting ;
Humbled before the prophet's knee,
He groaned, " Be injured Israel free !"

To heaven the sage upraised his wand ;
Back rolled the deluge from the land ;
Back to its caverns sank the gale ;
Fled from the noon the vapors pale ;
Broad burned again the joyous sun :
The hour of wrath and death was done.

THE FIRST-BORN OF EGYPT.

When life is forgot, and night hath power,
  And mortals feel no dread,
When silence and slumber rule the hour,
  And dreams are round the head ;
God shall smite the first born of Egypt's race ;
The destroyer shall enter each dwelling-place—
  Shall enter and choose his dead.

" To your homes," said the leader of Israel's host,
  " And slaughter a sacrifice :
" Let the life-blood be sprinkled on each door-post,
  " Nor stir till the morning arise :
And the angel of vengeance shall past you by,
" He shall see the red stain, and shall not come nigh,
  " Where the hope of your household lies. "

The people hear, and they bow them low—
  Each to his house hath flown :
The lamb is slain, and with blood they go,
  And sprinkle the lintel-stone ;
And the doors they close when the sun hath set,
But few in oblivious sleep forget
  The judgment to be done.

'Tis midnight—yet they hear no sound
  Along the lone still street ;
No blast of petilence sweeps the ground,
  No tramp of unearthly feet ;

Nor rush as of harpy wing goes by,
But the calm moon floats on the cloudless sky,
   'Mid her wan light clear and sweet.

Once only, shot like an arrowy ray,
   A pale blue flash was seen,
It pass'd so swift, the eye scarce could say
   That such a thing had been ;
Yet the beat of every heart was still,
And the flesh crawled fearfully and chill,
   And back flowed every vein.

The courage of Israel's bravest quail'd
   At the view of that awful light,
Though knowing the blood of their off'ring avail'd
   To shield them from its might;
They felt 'twas the Spirit of Death had past,
That the brightness they saw, his cold glance had cast
   On Egypt's land that night.

That his fearful eye had unwarn'd struck down,
   In the darkness of the grave,
The hope of that empire, the pride of its crown,
   The first-born of lord and slave ;—
The lovely, the tender, the ardent, the gay ;
Where are they ?—all wither'd in ashes away,
   At the terrible death-glare it gave.

From the couches of slumber ten thousand cries
   Burst forth 'mid the silence of dread—
The youth by his living brother lies,
   Sightless, and dumb, and dead !
The infant lies cold at his mother's breast :
She had kissed him alive, as she sank to rest ;
   She awakens—his life hath fled.

And shrieks from the palace-chambers break—
   Their inmates are steeped in woe,
And Pharaoh has found his arm too weak
   To arrest the mighty blow :
Wail, king of the Pyramids ! Egypt's throne
Cannot lighten thy heart of a single groan,
   For thy kingdom's heir laid low.

Wail, king of the Pyramids ! Death hath cast
   His shafts through thine empire wide,
But o'er Israel in bondage his rage hath past,
   No first-born of her's hath died—
Go, Satrap ! command that the captive be free,
Lest their God in fierce anger should smite even thee,
   On the crown of thy purple pride.

THE PASSAGE OF THE RED SEA.

FULL many a coal-black tribe and cany spear,
The hireling guards of Misraim's throne, were there.
From distant Cush they trooped, a warrior train,
Sirvah's green isle and Sennaar's marly plain :
On either wing their fiery coursers check
The parched and sinewy sons of Amalek :
While close behind, inured to feast on blood,
Deck'd in Behemoth's spoils, the tall Shangalla strode.
'Mid blazing helms and bucklers rough with gold,
Saw ye how swift the scythed chariots rolled ?
Lo, these are they, whom, lords of Afric's fates,
Old Thebes had poured through all her hundred gates,
Mother of armies!—How the emeralds glowed,
Where, flushed with power and vengeance, Pharaoh rode !
And stoled in white, those brazen wheels before,
Osiris' ark his swarthy wizards bore ;
And, still responsive to the trumpet's cry,
The priestly sistrum murmured—Victory !—
Why swell these shouts that rend the desert's gloom ?
Why come ye forth to combat ? warriors, whom ?
These flocks and herds, this faint and weary train
Red from the scourge, and recent from the chain ?
God of the poor, the poor and friendless save !
Giver and Lord of freedom, help the slave !
North, south, and west, the sandy whirlwinds fly,.
The circling horns of Egypt's chivalry.
On earth's last margin throng the weeping train :
Their cloudy guide moves on, "and must we swim the main?"
'Mid the light spray their snorting camels stood,
Nor bathed a fetlock in the nauseous flood,
He comes, their leader comes ! the man of, God,
O'er the wide waters lifts his mighty rod,
And onward treads : the circling waves retreat,
In hoarse, deep murmurs, from his holy feet;
And the chased surges, inly roaring, show
The hard wet sand and coral hills below.
 With limbs that falter and with hearts that swell,.
Down, down they pass a steep and slippery dell,
Around them rise, in pristine chaos hurl'd,
The ancient rocks, the secrets of the world ;
And flowers that blush beneath the ocean green,
And caves, the sea-calves' low-roofed haunt are seen.
Down, safely down the narrow pass they tread ;
The beetling waters storm above their head :
While far behind retires the sinking day,.
And fades on Edom's hills its latest ray.

Yet not from Israel fled the friendly light,
Or dark to them, or cheerless, came the night.
Still in their van, along that dreadful road,
Blazed broad and fierce the brandished sword of God.
Its meteor glare a tenfold lustre gave,
On the long mirror of the rosy wave :
While its blest beams a sunlike heat supply,
Warm every cheek, and dance in every eye.
To them alone, for Misraim's wizard train
Invoke for light their monster-gods in vain :
Clouds heaped on clouds their struggling sight confine,
And tenfold darkness broods above their line.
Yet on they fare, by reckless vengeance led,
And range unconscious through the ocean's bed,
Till midway now, that strange and fiery form
Showed his dread visage, lightening through the storm :
With withering splendour blasted all their might,
And brake their chariot-wheels, and marred their courser's
　　flight.
" Fly, Misraim, fly ! " The ravenous floods they see,
And fiercer than the floods, the Deity.
" Fly, Misraim, fly ! " From Edom's coral strand
Again the Prophet stretched his dreadful wand :
With one wild crash the thundering waters sweep,
And all is waves, a dark and lonely deep—
Yet o'er these lonely waves such murmurs past,
As mortal wailing swelled the nightly blast :
And strange and sad, the whispering surges bore
The groans of Egypt to Arabia's shore.
　　Oh ! welcome came the morn, where Israel stood
In trustless wonder by the avenging flood !
Oh ! welcome came the cheerful morn, to show
The drifted wreck of Zoan's pride below ;
The mangled limbs of men, the broken car,
A few sad relics of a nation's war :
Alas, how few ! Then soft as Elim's well,
The precious tears of new-born freedom fell.
And he, whose hardened heart alike had borne
The house of bondage. and the oppressor's scorn,
The stubborn slave, by hope's new beams subdued,
In faltering accents sobbed his gratitude—
Till, kindling into warmer zeal, around
The virgin timbrel waked its silver sound :
And in fierce joy no more by doubt supprest,
The struggling spirit throbbed in Miriam's breast.
She, with bare arms, and fixing on the sky
The dark transparence of her lucid eye,
Poured on the winds of heaven her wild sweet harmony.
" Where now," she sang, " the tall Egyptian spear ? .
" On's sunlike shield, and Zoan's chariot, where ?
" Above their ranks the whelming waters spread.

"Shout, Israel, for the Lord hath triumphèd!"
And every pause between, as Miriam sang,
From tribe to tribe the martial thunder rang;
And loud and far their stormy chorus spread,
"Shout, Israel, for the Lord hath triumphèd!"

THE SONG OF MIRIAM.

HARK to the sound of the timbrel,
   By the side of Egypt's waters;
'Tis the song and the dance of triumph,
   Of Israel's dark eyed daughters:
O'er many a neck so swan-like,
   The loose black locks are flowing;
And many a lip is smiling,
   And many a cheek is glowing;
And those dark eyes are beaming,
   And those warm hearts are leaping;
And those light forms are swimming,
   The measured dance-step keeping:
     And this is the song,
     As they sail along,
  Miriam, Miriam leads the throng!

"Oh, sing to Jehovah! who gloriously,
  Hath triumph'd, hath triumph'd, and no one but He;
Oh, sing! for Jehovah, victoriously,
  The horse and his rider hath sunk in the sea!"

Now the heights of Pi-hahiroth
   Catch the echo softly beating;
Now the rocks of Baal-zephon
   Answer to the light retreating;
Now across the sunny ocean,
   Floats the music of soft voices;
And above, the sky is cloudless,
   As if Nature's self rejoices:
And the song is sweetly sounding,
   And the step is lightly twining,
And the timbrel gaily ringing,
   And the eye with pleasure shining.

"Oh, sing to Jehovah! who gloriously,
  Hath triumph'd, hath triumph'd, and no one but He;
Oh, sing! for Jehovah, victoriously,
  The horse and his rider hath sunk in the sea!"

BALAAM.

He waved his wand, dark spirits knew
    That rod. Yet none obeyed its call;
And twice the mystic sign he drew,
    And twice beheld them bootless all;
Then knew, the seer, Jehovah's hand
And crushed the scroll, and broke the wand.

"I feel Him like a burning fire —
    When I would curse, my lips are dumb;.
But from those lips, 'mid hate and ire
    Unchecked the words of blessing come;
They come — and on His people rest
A people by the curser blest:

I see them from the mountain top,
    How fair their dwellings on the plain,
Like trees that crown the valley's slope,
    Like waves that glitter on the main!
Strong, strong the lion slumbering there —
Who first shall rouse him from his lair?

Crouch, Amelek! and thou, vain king!
    Crouch by thine altars — vainer still!
Hear ye the royal shouts that ring
    From Israel's camp beneath the hill?
They have a God amidst their tents;
Banner at once and battlements!

A star shall break through yonder skies,
    And beam on every nation's sight;
From yonder ranks a sceptre rise,
    And bow the nations to its might:
I see their glorious strength afar —
All hail, mild sceptre! hail, bright star!

And who am I, for whom is flung
    Aside the shrouding veil of time?
The seer whose rebel soul is rung
    By wrath, and prophesy, and crime:
The future as the past I see —
Woe, then, for Moab! woe for me."

On Peor's top the wizard stood,
    Around him Moab's princes bowed;
He bade — and altars streamed with blood
    And incense wrapped him like a shroud,
But vain the rites of earth and hell —
He spake — a mastered oracle!

SISERA.

"Why comes he not? why comes he not,
  My brave and noble son?
Why comes he not with his warlike men,
  And the trophies his sword has won?
How slowly roll his chariot-wheels!
  How weary is the day!
Pride of thy mother's lonely heart,
  Why dost thou still delay?

He comes not yet! will he never come
  To gladden these heavy eyes,
That have watched and watched from morn till eve,
  And again till the sun did rise?
Shall I greet no more his look of joy,
  Nor hear his manly voice?
Why comes he not with the spoils of war,
  And the damsels of his choice?"

Years rushed along in their ceaseless course,
  But Sisera came no more,
With his "mighty men" and his captive maids,
  As he oft had come before.
A woman's hand had done the deed
  That laid a hero low;—
A woman's heart had felt the grief
  That childless mothers know.

JEPHTHAH.

Rejoice, ye tribes of Israel, the Lord was on your side,
Your fierce and daring enemies have fallen in their pride.
In vain the heathen strove against Jehovah's awful word,
For Ammon's proud presumptuous sons have perished by the
  sword.

From Aroer to Minnith and to Abel's fertile plain,
Of twenty noble cities the "mighty men" are slain;
Rejoice, thou son of Gilead, the Lord hath heard thy vow,—
Thy foes are crushed, thy fathers' sons before thy presence bow.

It is an hour of triumph to the warrior of his band,
An hour of stern rejoicing to all the chosen land,
When the conqueror of Ammon, the valiant of his race,
Beholds once more with well-earned joy his long-lost native place.

But who is this advancing with gay attendant crowd ?
Oh ! Jephthah ! dost remember now the vow that thou hast vowed ?
Why is thy face so ghastly pale ? why sinks thy noble head ?
Thy daughter's blood must now atone for all that thou hast shed !

Honour and pomp and victory are all forgotten now,
And clouds of darkest anguish sweep across the father's brow,
He speaks—his words are words of death : he orders—is obeyed—
And lonely mountains mourn the fate of Israel's queenly maid.

Rejoice, ye tribes of Israel, the Lord was on your side,
Your fierce, presumptuous enemies have fallen in their pride !
But, Jephthah, thou art childless now, lift up thy voice and weep !
No sound of wailing can disturb thy daughter's dreamless sleep !

JEPHTHAH'S DAUGHTER.

Since our Country, our God — oh, my sire !
Demand that thy daughter expire ;
Since thy triumph was bought by thy vow —
Strike the bosom that's bared for thee now !

And the voice of my mourning is o'er,
And the mountains behold me no more :
If the hand that I love lay me low,
There cannot be pain in the blow !

And of this, O my father ! be sure —
That the blood of thy child is as pure
As the blessing I beg ere it flow,
And the last thought that soothes me below.

Though the virgins of Salem lament,
Be the judge and the hero unbent !
I have won the great battle for thee,
And my father and country are free !

When this blood of thy giving hath gush'd,
When the voice that thou lovest is hush'd,
Let my memory still be thy pride,
And forget not I smiled as I died!

SAMSON'S LAMENT FOR THE LOSS OF HIS SIGHT.

C Loss of sight, of thee I most complain!
Blind among enemies, O worse than chains,
Dungeon, or beggary, or decrepit age!
Light, the prime work of God, to me's extinct,
And all her various objects of delight
Annulled, which might in part my grief have eased,
Inferior to the vilest now become
Of man or worm; the vilest here excel me:
They creep, yet see; I, dark in light, exposed
To daily fraud, contempt, abuse, and wrong,
Within doors, or without, still as a fool,
In power of others, never in my own;
Scarce half I seem to live, dead more than half.
O dark, dark, dark, amid the blaze of noon,
Irrecoverably dark, total eclipse,
Without all hope of day!
O first created beam, and thou great Word,
Let there be light, and light was over all;
Why am I thus bereaved thy prime decree?
The sun to me is dark,
And silent as the moon,
When she deserts the night,
Hid in her vacant interlunar cave!
Since light so necessary is to life,
And almost life itself, if it be true
That light is in the soul,
She all in every part; why was the sight
To such a tender ball as the eye confined,
So obvious and so easy to be quenched?
And not, as feeling, through all parts diffused,
That she might look, at will, through every pore?
Then had I not been thus exiled from light,
As in the land of darkness, yet in light,
To live a life half dead, a living death,
And buried; but O, yet more miserable!
Myself my sepulchre, a moving grave!
Buried, yet not exempt

By privilege of death and burial
From worst of other evils, pains, and wrongs;
But made hereby obnoxious more
To all the miseries of life,
Life in captivity.

HANNAH AND SAMUEL.

THE rose was in rich bloom on Sharon's plain,
When a young mother, with her First-born thence
Went up to Zion; for the boy was vow'd
Unto the temple-service. By the hand
She led him, and her silent soul, the while,
Oft as the dewy laughter of his eye
Met her sweet serious glance, rejoic'd to think
That aught so pure, so beautiful, was hers,
To bring before her God.
     So pass'd they on,
O'er Judah's hills; and wheresoe'er the leaves
Of the broad sycamore made sounds at noon,
Like lulling rain-drops or the olive-boughs,
With their cool dimness, cross'd the sultry blue
Of Syria's heaven, she paus'd that he might rest;
Yet from her own meek eyelids chas'd the sleep
That weigh'd their dark fringe down, to sit and watch
The crimson deepening o'er his cheek's repose,
As at a red flower's heart: and where a fount
Lay, like a twilight star, midst palmy shades,
Making its banks green gems along the wild,
There too she linger'd, from the diamond wave
Drawing clear water for his rosy lips,
And softly parting clusters of jet curls,
To bathe his brow.
     At last the Fane was reach'd,
The earth's One Sanctuary; and rapture hush'd
Her bosom, as before her, thro' the day
It rose, a mountain of white marble, steep'd
In light like floating gold.—But when that hour
Waned to the farewell moment, when the boy
Lifted, through rainbow-gleaming tears, his eye
Beseechingly to hers, and, half in fear,
Turn'd from the white-rob'd priest, and round her arm
Clung e'en as ivy clings; the deep spring-tide
Of nature then swell'd high; and o'er her child
Bending, her soul brake forth in mingled rounds
Of weeping and sad song.—" Alas!" she cried,

" Alas, my boy ! thy gentle grasp is on me,
The bright tears quiver in thy pleading eyes,
   And now fond thoughts arise,
And silver cords again to earth have won me,
And like a vine thou claspest my full heart—
   How shall I hence depart ?

How the lone paths retrace, where thou wert playing
So late along the mountain at my side ?
   And I, in joyous pride,
By every place of flowers my course delaying,
Wove, e'en as pearls, the lilies, round thy hair,
   Beholding thee so fair !

And oh! the home whence thy bright smile hath parted !
Will it not seem as if the sunny day
   Turn'd from its door away,
While, thro' its chambers wandering weary-hearted,
I languish for thy voice, which, past me still,
   Went like a singing rill ?

Under the palm-trees, thou no more shalt meet me,
When from the fount at evening I return,
   With the full water-urn !
Nor will thy sleep's low, dove like murmurs greet me,
As midst the silence of the stars I wake,
   And watch for thy dear sake.

And thou, will slumber's dewy cloud fall round thee,
Without thy mother's hand to smooth thy bed ?
   Wilt thou not vainly spread
Thine arms, when darkness as a veil hath wound thee,
To fold my neck ; and lift up, in thy fear,
   A cry which none shall hear ?

What have I said, my child ?—will HE not hear thee,
Who the young ravens heareth from their nest ?
   Will HE not guard thy rest,
And, in the hush of holy midnight near thee,
Breathe o'er thy soul, and fill its dreams with joy ?
   Thou shalt sleep soft, my boy !

I give thee to thy God !—the God that gave thee,
A well-spring of deep gladness to my heart !
   And precious as thou art,
And pure as dew of Hermon, He shall have thee,
My own, my beautiful, my undefiled !
   And thou shalt be His child !

Therefore, farewell ! I go ; my soul may fail me,
As the stag panteth for the water-brooks,

Yearning for thy sweet looks !
But thou my First-born ! droop not nor bewail me,
Thou in the shadow of the Rock shalt dwell,
The Rock of Strength—Farewell ! "

THE CHILD SAMUEL.

Hushed was the evening hymn,
   The temple courts were dark ;
   The lamp was burning dim
   Before the sacred Ark,
When suddenly a voice divine
Rang through the silence of the shrine.

   The old man meek and mild,
   The priest of Israel slept ;
   His watch the temple child,
   The little Levite kept ;
And what from Eli's sense was sealed,
The Lord to Hannah's son revealed.

   O give me Samuel's ear,
   The open ear, O Lord,
   Alive and quick to hear
   Each whisper of Thy word ;
Like him to answer at Thy call,
And so obey Thee first of all.

   O give me Samuel's heart,
   A lowly heart that waits,
   Where in Thy house Thou art,
   Or watches at Thy gates ;
By day and night, a heart that still
Moves at the breathing of Thy will.

   O give me Samuel's mind,
   A sweet, unmurmuring faith,
   Obedient and resigned
   To Thee in life and death ;
That I may read with child-like eyes,
Truths that are hidden from the wise.

DAVID AND GOLIATH.

When Israel's host in Elah's valley lay,
O'erwhelm'd with shame, and trembling with dismay,
They saw how fierce Goliath proudly trod
Before their ranks and braved the living God.
  On Israel's ranks he cast a withering look,
And Elah's valley trembled as he spoke.

  " Ye slaves of Saul, why thus in proud parade
Of martial threatening, stand your ranks arrayed ?
Though high your vaults, and unsubdued your pride,
A single arm the contest may decide.
Send forth the best and bravest of your hosts,
To prove in me what might Philistia boasts ;
And if your champion fall beneath my hand,
Let Israel own Philistia's high command :
But if his better arm the triumph gain,
Her yielding sons shall wear the victor's chain.
You, and your God who rules the cloudy sky,
Armies of Israel I this day defy !"

  Through Israel's curdling veins cold horror ran,
And each sunk warrior felt no longer man :
One heart alone its wonted fire retains,
One heart alone the giant's threats disdains :
David, the last of Jesse's numerous race,
Deep in his bosom feels the dire disgrace,
That e'er a godless Philistine, so proud,
His single prowess thus should vaunt aloud.

  Before his prince, magnanimous he stands,
And lifts the imploring eye and suppliant hands,
With modest grace to let him prove the fight,
And die or conquer in his country's right.
  The king and nobles with attention hung
To hear the aspirings of a mind so young,
But deem his darings, in the unequal strife,
Were but a fond and useless waste of life.

  Then David thus : " As erst my flocks I kept,
Pale shone the moon-beam, and the hamlet slept ;
In that still hour a shaggy bear I spied
Snuff the night gale, and range the valley-side ;
He seized a lamb,—and by this hand he died.
And when a lion, made by hunger bold,
From Jordan's swelling streams o'erleap'd the fold ;
The brindled savage in my hands I tore,

Caught by the beard, and crush'd him in his gore.
The God that saved me from the infuriate boar
And famish'd lion still has power to spare ;
And something whispers, if the strife I meet,
Soon shall the boaster fall beneath my feet."

Moved by his words the king and chieftains yield ;
His spirit laud, and arm him for the field :
In royal mail his youthful limbs they dress'd,
The greaves, the corslet, shield, and threatening crest.

But ill those youthful limbs with arms accord.
And ill that hand can wield the imperial sword ;
Whence wisdom cautions—these to lay aside,
And choose the arms whose power he oft had tried.
Straight in his hand the well-proved sling he took,
And in his scrip five pebbles from the brook ;
These all his earthly arms :—but o'er his head,
Had Faith divine her sheltering ægis spread.
His bosom beats with generous ardour high,
And new-born glories kindle in his eye ;
Swift o'er the field he bounds with vigour light,
Marks the gigantic foe, and claims the fight.

Now men of Israel, pour your ardent prayer :
" God of our fathers, to thy sovereign care
We trust our champion, for to Thee belong
Strength for the weak, and weakness for the strong:
Arm him with might to vindicate Thy name,
To smite the proud, and blot out Israel's shame ;
Let angels round him spread the guardian shield,
And oh ! restore in triumph from the field !"

Philistia's chief now mark'd with high disdain,
The light-arm'd stripling rushing to the plain ;
Saw, with a scornful smile his airy tread,
And downy cheek suffused with rosy red ;
His pliant limbs not cased in shining mail,
No shield to ward, no sabre to assail ;
But clad like shepherd-swain,—when swains advance
To hand the fair, and frolic in the dance.
Fierce from his breast the growling thunder broke,
And Elah's valley trembled as he spoke.

" O powerful Dagon ! wherefore was I born ?
Am I a dog ?—the theme of children's scorn ?
Cursed be thy God ! cursed thou presumptuous boy !
But come—draw nigh—and glut my furious joy.
Thy feeble body, crush'd beneath my power,
The birds shall mangle, and the dogs devour."

Then Jesse's son :—" Accoutred for the field,
Proudly thou marchest with thy spear and shield :
But I unarm'd, yet, reckless of thy boasts,
Approach, protected by the God of Hosts ;
That righteous power, whom thy infuriate pride,
With tongue blaspheming, has this day defied.
Me, of our race the humblest, has He sped,
From thy broad trunk to lop thy impious head,
And through thy armies wasting vengeance spread ;—
That all may know, through earth's wide realms abroad,
To trust the righteous cause to Israel's God.
He saves not by the shield, by spears, or swords :—
No more.—Advance—the battle is the Lord's."

With giant stride the lowering foe draws nigh,
Strength in his arm, and fury in his eye ;
In thought, already gives the ruthless wound,
And the scorn'd youth transfixes to the ground.
While David, rapid as the fleetest wing,
Whirls round his head the quick revolving sling ;
Aims with experienced eye, the avenging blow
At the broad visage of the advancing foe.—
How booms the thong, impatient to be free,
Wing'd with resistless speed, and arm'd with destiny !—
'Tis gone—loud whizzing flies the ponderous stone !—
That dirge of death—hark ! heard ye Dagon groan ?
It strikes—it crashes through the fractured bone !
Struck in his full career, the giant feels
The bolt of death;—his mountain-body reels—
And nerveless, headlong, thunders to the ground.—
Loud bursts of joy along the vale resound :
Shout ! men of Israel, shout—till earth and sky,
With replication loud, re-echo victory !
See, see him now, as flushed with honest pride,
He draws the sabre from the giant's side :
Now on the groaning trunk behold him tread,
And from the shoulders lop the ghastly head !

Shout, men of Israel, shout your hero's praise !
Send it immortal down to future days !
Let farthest Dan his triumph loud proclaim
And Sheba's springs resound his glorious name ;
In Jesse's son, O Bethlehem ! rejoice ;
And Salem, thou exalt thy grateful voice ;
Thy victor hail triumphant in the Lord ;
Girt with the grisly spoils, he waves the reeking sword

Daughters of Israel, loud his praises sing !
With harp and timbrel hail your future king.
By mighty Saul a thousand bite the plain,
But mightier David has ten thousand slain !

SAUL AND DAVID.

Deep was the furrow in the royal brow,
When David's hand, lightly as vernal gales
Rippling the brook of Kedron, skimmed the lyre;
He sang of Jacob's youngest son, the child
Of his old age, sold to the Ishmaelite;
His exaltation to the second power
In Pharaoh's realm; his brethren thither sent;
Suppliant they stood before his face — well known,
Unknowing — till Joseph fell upon the neck
Of Benjamin, his mother's son, and wept.
Unconsciously the warlike shepherd paused;
But when he saw, down the yet quivering string,
The tear-drop trembling glide, abashed, he checked,
Indignant at himself, the bursting flood,
And, with a sweep impetuous, struck the chords.
From side to side his hands traversely glance
Like lightning 'thwart a stormy sea; his voice
Arises 'mid the clang, and straightway calms
The harmonious tempest to a solemn swell,
Majestical, triumphant, for he sings
Of Arad's mighty host by Israel's arms
Subdued; of Israel through the desert led
He sings; of him who was their leader, called
By God Himself from keeping Jethro's flock
To be a ruler o'er the chosen race.
Kindles the eye of Saul: his arm is poised; —
Harmless the javelin quivers in the wall.

SAUL IN THE CAVE OF ENGEDI.

Stay, stay, injurious king; oh, father stay,
If I may yet so style thee; why dost thou
Listen to those who say I am disloyal?
Lo, in this hour, and in this very cave,
How easily could I have ta'en your life;
As some did bid me do, but I refrained,
"I will not harm," I said, "the Lord's Anointed."
In proof of which behold here your robe's skirt,
Which sole I took, yet could as easily
Have ta'en your life as it. Yes, look on this
Upbraiding proof; yes, look on this dumb witness,

Then stand convicted of injustice toward me.
Believe, oh, cruel and suspicious king,
That since I took but this and spared your life,—
At last, believe me honest. Oh, my father,
Why hast thou ever deemed that I was other?
Why dost thou hunt me like a beast o' th' forest?
Let the Lord judge between us; let the Lord
Be mine Avenger: for I will not harm thee.
Oh, that your majesty should have dread of me!—
Have dread of one so poor and weak as I!
For what could I do (even were I so minded)
Against your majesty? But I will nothing:
Let the Lord judge between us; let Him enquire;
Yes, let Him plead my cause still with your anger;
Let Him from it at length deliver me.

SAUL AND THE WITCH OF ENDOR.

Thou, whose spell can raise the dead,
Bid the prophet's form appear—
"Samuel, raise thy buried head!—
King, behold the phantom seer!"
Earth yawned; he stood, the centre of a cloud;
Light changed its hue, returning from his shroud;
Death stood all glassy in his fixèd eye;
His hand was withered and his veins were dry;
His foot, in bony whiteness, glittered there,
Shrunken and sinewless, and ghastly bare;
From lips that moved not, and unbreathing frame,
Like caverned winds, the hollow accents came.
Saul saw, and fell to earth as falls the oak
At once when blasted by the thunder stroke.
 "Why is my sleep disquieted?
Who is he that calls the dead?
Is it thou—oh king? Behold
Bloodless are these limbs and cold:
Such are mine, and such shall be
Thine to-morrow when with me;
Ere the coming day is done,
Such shalt thou be, such thy son.
Fare thee well, but for a day;
Then we mix our mouldering clay;—
Thou, thy race, lie pale and low,
Pierced by shafts of many a bow;
And the falchion by thy side
To thy heart thy hand shall guide;
Crownless, breathless, headless fall
Son and Sire, the house of Saul!"

THE THREE MIGHTY MEN

On the hill by Bethlehem David stood,
   He and his warriors bold,
And their dark eyes flashed as they looked below,
   For the Philistines held the hold.

But the hero laid aside the spear,
   And sat him on the hill;
And, looking on his native town,
   His eyes began to fill.

He thought of the happy evening hours
   When, ere the sun went down,
The maidens, to the gushing well,
   Passed through the ancient town.

And sighed, "Oh, would that I now could drink
   As in that happy state,
A draught from the well of Bethlehem
   That is beside the gate!" . . . .

Then the three mighty men arose,
   Adino the Tachmonite,
Eleazar the son of Dodo,
   And Shammah the Hararite;

They spake not a word, but each seized his spear,
   And buckled his helmet on,
And the whole host watched their steps, till they
   Adown the hill were gone.

But soon the smiting of swords was heard,
   And the clash of spears arose,
And the three in the open gate appeared,
   Begirt with Philistine foes.

They slew to the right and slew to the left,
   And ever they slew before,
And backward through the bloody street
   The struggling crowd they bore,

Until they came to the deep, deep well,
   And there they turned and stayed;
And wiping his sword on the bearded grass
   Adino the Tachmonite said:

"Now stand ye two before the well,
   And fight the foe amain;

And I will let the bucket down
  And draw it up again."

And so did he, and so did they,
  And when the work was sped,
He took the spear in his good right hand,
  And the pitcher on his head.

And then when the three looked down, and saw
  The iron-girt array
Of Ekronites and Ashdodites,
  That filled the gleaming way,

They prayed to the God of Israel,
  To gird their loins with might,
To clothe their swords with thunder,
  And teach their hands to fight.

There was many a noble warrior there,
  From many an ancient town,
But of all the host could none hold his place,
  When the three came rushing down :

They slew to the right, and they slew to the left,
  And still they slew before,
And ever their shout " Immanu-El !"
  Was heard through the battles' roar.

The shield and helm they split in twain,
  And broke the breast of mail,
And every blow of their falchions rang
  Far o'er the Giants' Vale ;

And many a lord of the Philistines
  Was slain upon that day,
And Rephaim and Anakim
  Lay trodden in the way ;

Until through the uncircumcised
  A bloody way they clave,
And hear the shout of victory
  Their glad companions gave,

Until they brought to the spreading oak,
  Where the son of Jessè sate,
The draught from the well of Bethlehem
  That is beside the gate !

. . . .

King David took the pitcher
  From brave Adino's hand,
But he saw on his helm the deep dints made
  By many a hostile brand ;

And he saw on the arm of Shammah
  Big gouts of blood appear,
And he saw on Eleazar's breast
  The cut of a brazen spear.

He took the water from his lips
  And poured it where he stood —
"Nay, God forbid that I should drink
  Of water that's bought with blood!

These men have bought it with their life,
  Have won it with their sword!
I will not drink it — it shall be
  An offering to the Lord!"

DAVID'S LAMENTATION OVER HIS SICK CHILD.

" Twas daybreak, and the fingers of the dawn
Drew the night's curtain, and touched silently
The eyelids of the king. And David woke
And robed himself, and prayed. The inmates, now
Of the vast palace were astir, and feet
Glided along the tesselated floors
With a pervading murmur, and the fount
Whose music had been all the night unheard,
Played as if light had made it audible :
And each one, waking, blessed it unaware.
  The fragrant strife of sunshine with the morn
Sweetened the air to ecstasy! and now
The king's wont was to lie upon his couch
Beneath the sky-roof of the inner court,
And, shut in from the world, but not from heaven,.
Play with his loved son by the fountain's lip ;
For, with idolatry confessed alone—
To the rapt wires of his reproofless harp,
He loved the child of Bathsheba. And when
The golden selvedge of his robe was heard
Sweeping the marble pavement, from within
Broke forth a child's laugh suddenly, and words
Articulate, perhaps, to *his* heart only,
Pleading to come to him. They brought the boy,.
An infant cherub, leaping as if used
To hover with that motion upon wings,
And marvellously beautiful! His brow
Had the inspired up-lift of the king's,

And kingly was his infantine regard ;
But his ripe mouth was of the ravishing mould
Of Bathsheba's—the hue and type of love,
Rosy and passionate—and oh, the moist
Unfathomable blue of his large eyes
Gave out its light as twilight shows a star,
And drew the heart of the beholder in !—
And this was like his mother.
                David's lips
Moved with unuttered blessings, and awhile
He closed the lids upon his moistened eyes,
And, with the round cheek of the nestling boy
Pressed to his bosom, sat as if afraid
That but the lifting of his lids might jar
His heart's cup from its fulness. Unobserved,
A servant of the outer court had knelt
Waiting before him ; and a cloud the while
Had rapidly spread o'er the summer heaven ;
And, as the chill of the withdrawing sun
Fell on the king, he lifted up his eyes
And frowned upon the servant—for that hour
Was hallowed to his heart and his fair child,
And none might seek him. And the king arose,
And with a troubled countenance looked up
To the fast gathering darkness; and, behold,
The servant bowed himself to earth, and said,
" Nathan the prophet cometh from-the Lord ! "
And David's lips grew white, and with a clasp
Which wrung a murmur from the frighted child,
He drew him to his breast, and covered him
With the long foldings of his robe, and said,
" I will come forth. Go now !" And lingeringly,
With kisses on the fair uplifted brow,
And mingled words of tenderness and prayer
Breaking in tremulous accents from his lips,
He gave to them the child, and bowed his head
Upon his breast with agony. And so,
To hear the errand of the man of God,
He fearfully went forth. . . . .

It was the morning of the seventh day.
A hush was in the palace, for all eyes
Had woke before the morn : and they who drew
The curtains to let in the welcome light,
Moved in their chambers with unslippered feet,
And listened breathlessly. And still no stir !
The servants who kept watch without the door
Sat motionless ; the purple casement-shades
From the low windows had been rolled away,
To give the child air, and the flickering light
That, all the night, within the spacious court,

Had drawn the watchers' eyes to one spot only,
Paled with the sunrise and fled in.
      And hushed
With more than stillness was the room where lay
The king's son on his mother's breast. His locks
Slept at the lips of Bathsheba unstirred—
So fearfully, with heart and pulse kept down,
She watched his breathless slumber. The low moan
That from his lips all night broke fitfully,
Had silenced with the daybreak ; and a smile,
Or something that would fain have been a smile,
Played in his parted mouth ; and though his lids
Hid not the blue of his unconscious eyes,
His senses seemed all peacefully asleep,
And Bathsheba in silence blessed the morn
That brought back hope to her. But when the king
Heard not the voice of the complaining child,
Nor breath from out the room, nor foot astir—
But morning there—so welcomeless and still—
He groaned and turned upon his face. The nights
Had wasted, and the mornings come, and days
Crept through the sky, unnumbered by the king,
Since the child sickened ; and without the door,
Upon the bare earth prostrate, he had lain,
Listening only to the moons that brought
Their inarticulate tidings, and the voice
Of Bathsheba, whose pity and caress,
In loving utterance all broke with tears,
Spoke as his heart would speak if he were there,
And filled his prayer with agony. Oh God !
To Thy bright mercy-seat the way is far !
How fail the weak words while the heart keeps on !
And when the spirit, mournfully, at last,
Kneels at the throne—how cold—how distantly
The comforting of friends falls on the ear !—
The anguish they would speak to, gone to Thee !
But suddenly the watchers at the door
Rose up, and they who ministered within,
Crept to the threshold and looked earnestly
Where the king lay. And still, while Bathsheba
Held the unmoving child upon her knees,
The curtains were let down, and all came forth,
And, gathering with fearful looks apart,
Whispered together.
      And the king arose
And gazed on them a moment, and with voice
Of quick, uncertain utterance, he asked,
" Is the child dead ? " They answered, " he is dead."
But when they looked to see him fall again
Upon his face and rend himself and weep—
For, while the child was sick, his agony

Would bear no comforters, and they had thought
His heartstrings with the tidings must give way—
Behold ! his face grew calm, and, with his robe
Gathered together, like his kingly wont,
He silently went in.   And David came,
Robed and anointed, forth, and to the house
Of God went up to pray. And he returned,
And they set bread before him and he ate—
And when they marvelled, he said, *" Wherefor mourn ?*
The child is dead, and I shall go to him—
But he will not return to me."

ABSALOM.

THE waters slept. Night's silvery veil hung low
On Jordan's bosom, and the eddies curled
Their glassy rings beneath it, like the still
Unbroken beating of the sleeper's pulse.
The reeds bent down the stream : the willow-leaves,
With a soft cheek upon the lulling tide,
Forgot the lifting winds ; and the long stems,
Whose flowers the water, like a gentle nurse,
Bears on its bosom, quietly give way,
And leaned, in graceful attitudes, to rest.
How strikingly the course of nature tells,
By its light heed of human suffering,
That it was fashioned for a happier world !

    King David's limbs were weary. He had fled
From far Jerusalem : and now he stood,
With his faint people, for a little rest
Upon the shore of Jordan. The light wind
Of morn was stirring, and he bared his brow
To its refreshing breath ; for he had worn
The mourner's covering, and he had not felt
That he could see his people until now.
They gathered round him on the fresh green bank,
And spoke their kindly words ; and, as the sun
Rose up in heaven, he knelt among them there,
And bowed his head upon his hands to pray.
Oh ! when the heart is full—when bitter thoughts
Come crowding thickly up for utterance,
And the poor common words of courtesy
Are such a very mockery—how much
The bursting heart may pour itself in prayer !

He prayed for Israel ; and his voice went up
Strongly and fervently. He prayed for those
Whose love had been his shield ; and his deep tones
Grew tremulous. But oh ! for Absalom—
For his estranged, misguided Absalom—
The proud, bright being, who had burst away
In all his princely beauty, to defy
The heart that cherished him—for him he poured,
In agony that would not be controlled,
Strong supplication, and forgave him there,
Before his God, for his deep sinfulness.

* * * * * *

   The pall was settled. He who slept beneath
Was straightened for the grave ; and, as the folds
Sunk to the still proportions, they betrayed
The matchless symmetry of Absalom.
His hair was yet unshorn, and silken curls
Were floating round the tassels as they swayed
To the admitted air, as glossy now
As when in hours of gentle dalliance, bathing
The snowy fingers of Judea's girls.
His helm was at his feet : his banner, soiled
With trailing through Jerusalem, was laid
Reversed, beside him : and the jewelled hilt,
Whose diamonds lit the passage of his blade,
Rested, like mockery, on his covered brow.
The soldiers of the king trod to and fro,
Clad in the garb of battle ; and their chief,
The mighty Joab, stood beside the bier,
And gazed upon the dark pall steadfastly,
As if he feared the slumberer might stir.
A slow step startled him. He grasped his blade
As if a trumpet rang; but the bent form
Of David entered, and he gave command,
In a low tone to his few followers,
And left him with his dead. The King stood still
Till the last echo died : then throwing off
The sackcloth from his brow, and laying back
The pall from the still features of his child,
He bowed his head upon him, and broke forth
In the resistless eloquence of woe !—
" Alas ! my noble boy ! that thou shouldst die !
  Thou, who wert made so beautifully fair !
That death should settle in thy glorious eye,
  And leave his stillness in this clustering hair
How could he mark thee for the silent tomb,
  My proud boy, Absalom !

"Cold is thy brow, my son ! and I am chill,
  As to my bosom I have tried to press thee,

How was I wont to feel my pulses thrill,
    Like a rich harp-string, yearning to caress thee,
And hear thy sweet 'My Father,' from these dumb
    And cold lips, Absalom!

"The grave hath won thee. I shall hear the gush
    Of music, and the voices of the young;
And life will pass me in the mantling blush,
    And the dark tresses to the soft wind flung;
But thou no more, with thy sweet voice, shalt come
    To meet me, Absalom!

" And oh! when I am stricken, and my heart,
    Like a bruised reed, is waiting to be broken,
How will its love for thee, as I depart,
    Yearn for thine ear to drink its last deep token!
It were so sweet, amid death's gathering gloom,
    To see thee, Absalom!

" And now, farewell! 'Tis hard to give thee up,
    With death so like a gentle slumber on thee—
And thy dark sin!—Oh I could drink the cup,
    If from this woe its bitterness had won thee.
May God have called thee, like a wanderer, home,
    My erring Absalom!"

He covered up his face, and bowed himself
A moment on his child; then, giving him
A look of melting tenderness, he clasped
His hands convulsively, as if in prayer;
And, as a strength were given him of God,
He rose up calmly and composed the pall
Firmly and decently, and left him there,
As if his rest had been a breathing sleep.

TEMPLES.

How fair, in page of Holy Writ, Judea's Temple stands!
'Twas God himself who fashion'd it by means of mortal hands:
'Twas He conceiv'd the grand design—the gates—the massive
    wall;
The outer courts—the inner shrine—the "Holiest of all."

Majestical it rose beneath the Master-builder's eye,
And soon, within its courts, the breath of incense rose on high;

While priests, by altars stain'd with blood, were loud in praise
    and pray'r,
And over all, Shechinah stood to show that God was there.

That temple charms no more the sight—its stones are prostrate
    laid—
Its holy pomp, each solemn rite, were doom'd of old to fade:
They were but *shadows* of the things which Christians now
    possess—
The grey of early dawn which brings the Sun of Righteousness.

But God, our God, has Temples still, in which the faithful meet,
To hear their loving Master's will, and hymn His praises sweet,
'Tis there, their spirits seem to leave this world for one above,
As they the pledges sweet receive of Jesus' dying love.

ELIJAH'S INTERVIEW.

On Horeb's rock the prophet stood,—
    The Lord before him passed:
A hurricane in angry mood
    Swept by him strong and fast;
The forest fell before its force,
The rocks were shivered in its course:
    God was not in the blast;
'Twas but the whirlwind of His breath,
Announcing danger, wreck, and death.

It ceased. The air grew mute,—a cloud
    Came, muffling up the sun.
When, through the mountain, deep and loud
    An earthquake thundered on;
The frightened eagle sprang in air,
The wolf ran howling from his lair;
    God was not in the storm;
'Twas but the rolling of His car,
The tramping of His steeds from far.

'Twas still again,—and Nature stood
    And calmed her ruffled frame;
When swift from heaven a fiery flood
    To earth devouring came;
Down to the depth the ocean fled,—
The sickening sun looked wan and dead:
    Yet God filled not the flame;
'Twas but the terror of His eye,
That lightened through the troubled sky.

At last, a voice all still and small
    Rose sweetly on the ear;
Yet rose so shrill and clear, that all
    In heaven and earth might hear;

It spoke of peace, it spoke of love,
It spoke as angels speak above:
    And God himself was there;
For, O! it was a *Father's* voice,
That bade the trembling heart rejoice.

Speak, gracious Lord, speak ever thus,
    And let thy terrors prove
But harbingers of peace to us,
    But heralds of thy love;
Come through the earthquake, fire, and storm,
Come in thy mildest, sweetest form,
    And all our fears remove;
One word from Thee is all we claim—
Be that one word a Saviour's name!

ELISHA.

WHEN the lowly follower of the plough
    Received the highest call,
That man can hear in the world below,
    He left his earthly all;
And follow'd the steps of the man of God,
    With a true and steadfast heart;
Nor from his master, while earth he trod,
    Would the faithful servant part.

And noble was the gift he sought,
    In the sad parting hour;
A spirit with zeal for Jehovah fraught,
    And endued with heavenly power.
So blessed to behold the glorious blaze
    Of the chariot of fire;
Heard his ear some notes of heavenly praise,
    As it fell from seraph lyre?

None knows—but he read in the parting wave,
    Of that power, the earnest true,
That should lead him on, till beyond the grave,
    His master again he'd view:
And with spirit lifted above the world,

He to the warfare turned;
Sin's fair lures spread, or its fierce darts hurled,
Alike his armor spurned.

And the might of earthly kings and lords,
In the power of God defied;
Never fear could hush his burning words,
Or make him turn aside.
Even when he wept o'er Israel's doom,
His spirit was calm within,
Knowing the Lion of Judah would come
And vanquish the serpent Sin.

Though the light of that glorious day afar
Never gladdened his mortal eyes;
In his heart shone the beautiful Morning Star,
Illuminating faith's calm skies.
Through the waning night, and the weary strife,
He was true to his solemn trust:
Till he won in Heaven a crown of life,
And his dust returned to dust.

We own the blessings he waited for
With such unswerving faith;
But still we wage the ceaseless war,
Nor rest our arms till death,
Though no visible army's dread array
Calls us from ease to part;
There are ghostly foes that night and day
Assail the Christian's heart.
But, praise to Christ, though life be long,
When the vale of death we've trod,
We shall rest in bliss with the victor throng,
That surround the throne of God.

THE DESTRUCTION OF SENNACHERIB

The Assyrian came down like the wolf on the fold,
And his cohorts were gleaming in purple and gold;
And the sheen of their spears was like stars on the sea,
When the blue wave rolls nightly on deep Galilee.
Like the leaves of the forest when Summer is green,
That host with their banners at sunset were seen:
Like the leaves of the forest when Autumn hath blown,
That host on the morrow lay withered and strown.

For the Angel of Death spread his wings on the blast,
And breathed in the face of the foe as he passed;

And the eyes of the sleepers waxed deadly and chill,
And their hearts but once heaved, and for ever grew still!
And there lay the steed with his nostril all wide,
But through it there rolled not the breath of his pride,
And the foam of his gasping lay white on the turf,
And cold as the spray of the rock-beating surf.

And there lay the rider distorted and pale,
With the dew on his brow, and the rust on his mail,
And the tents were all silent, the banners alone,
The lances unlifted, the trumpet unblown.
And the widows of Ashur are loud in their wail,
And the idols are broke in the temple of Baal;
And the might of the Gentile, unsmote by the sword,
Hath melted like snow in the glance of the Lord!

CHORAL HYMN OF THE JEWISH MAIDENS.

King of kings! and Lord of lords!
  Thus we move, our sad steps timing,
  To our cymbal's feeblest chiming
Where Thy house its rest accords.
Chased and wounded birds are we,
Through the dark air fled to Thee;
To the shadow of Thy wings,
  Lord of lords! and King of kings!

Behold, O Lord! the heathen tread
  The branches of thy fruitful vine,
  That its luxurious tendrils spread
O'er all the hills of Palestine.
And now the wild boar comes to waste
Even us, the greenest bough and last
That, drinking of Thy choicest dew,
On Zion's hill in beauty grew.

No! by the marvels of Thine hand,
Thou still wilt save Thy chosen land;
By all Thy ancient mercies shown,
By all our fathers' foes o'erthrown;
By the Egyptian's car-borne host,
Scattered on the Red Sea coast;
By that wide and bloodless slaughter
Underneath the drowning water.

Like us in utter helplessness,
In their last and worst distress,—

On the sand and sea weed lying,
Israel poured her doleful sighing ;
While before the deep sea flowed,
And behind fierce Egypt rode—
To their fathers' God they prayed,
To the Lord of Hosts for aid.

On the margin of the flood
With lifted rod the prophet stood ;
And the summoned east wind blew,
And aside it sternly threw
The gathered waves, that took their stand,
Like crystal rocks, on either hand ;
Or walls of sea-green marble piled,
Round some irregular city wild.

Then the light of morning lay,
On the wonder-pavèd way,
Where the treasures of the deep
In their caves of coral sleep.
The profound abysses, where
Was never sound from upper air,
Rang with Israel's chanted words,
"King of kings ! and Lord of lords !"

Then with bow and banner glancing,
   On exulting Egypt came,
With her chosen horsemen prancing,
   And her cars on wheels of flame ;
In a rich and boastful ring
All around her furious king.
But the Lord from out His cloud,
The Lord looked down upon the proud ;
And the host drave heavily
Down the deep bosom of the sea.

With a quick and sudden swell
Prone the liquid ramparts fell;
Over horse and over car,
Over every man of war,
Over Pharaoh's crown of gold,
The loud thundering billows rolled.
As the level waters spread,
Down they sank, they sank like lead,
Down without a cry or groan.
And the morning sun that shone
On myriads of bright armèd men,
Its meridian radiance then
Cast on a wide sea, heaving as of yore,
Against a silent, solitary shore.

Then did Israel's maidens sing,
Then did Israel's trimbrels ring,
To Him, the King of kings! that in the sea,
The Lord of lords! had triumphed gloriously.
And our timbrels' flashing chords,
King of kings! and Lord of lords!
Shall they not attunèd be.

Once again to victory!
Lo! a glorious triumph now
  Lo! against Thy people come
A mightier Pharaoh! wilt not Thou
  Craze the chariot-wheels of Rome?
Will not, like the Red Sea wave,
  Thy stern anger overthrow?
And from worse than bondage save,
  From sadder than Egyptian woe,
Those whose silver cymbals glance,
Those who lead the suppliant dance;
Thy race, the only race that sings
"Lord of lords! and King of kings!"

JERUSALEM.

FALLEN is thy throne, O Israel!
  Silence is o'er thy plains!
Thy dwellings all lie desolate,
  Thy children weep in chains.
Where are the dews that fed thee
  On Etham's barren shore?
That fire from heaven that led thee
  Now lights thy path no more!

Lord, thou didst love Jerusalem;
  Once she was all thine own:
Her love thy fairest heritage,
  Her power thy glory's throne;
Till evil came and blighted
  Thy long-loved olive tree,
And Salem's shrines were lighted
  For other gods than Thee.

Then sank the star of Solyma,
  Then pass'd her glory's day,
Like heath that in the wilderness
  The light wind whirls away.
Silent and waste her bowers,

Where once the mighty trod,
And sunk those guilty towers
Where Baal reign'd as God.

"Go!" said the Lord, "ye conquerors,
Steep in her blood your swords,
And raze to earth her battlements,
For they are not the Lord's.
Tell Zion's mournful daughter
O'er kindred bones she'll tread,
And Hinnom's vale of slaughter
Shall hide but half her dead."

But soon shall other pictured scenes
In brighter vision rise,
When Zion's sun shall sevenfold shine
On all her mourners' eyes;
And on her mountains beauteous stand
The messengers of peace;
"Salvation by the Lord's right hand,"
They shout and never cease.

PALESTINE.

REFT of thy sons, amid thy foes forlorn,
Mourn, widow'd queen! forgotten Zion, mourn!
Is this thy place, sad city, this thy throne,
Where the wild desert rears its craggy stone?
While suns unbless'd their angry lustre fling,
And way-worn pilgrims seek the scanty spring?
Where now thy pomp, which kings with envy view'd?
Where now thy might, which all those kings subdued?
No martial myriads muster at thy gate;
No suppliant nations in thy temple wait;
No prophet-bards, the glittering courts among,
Wave the full lyre, and swell the tide of song;
But lawless Force and meagre Want are there,
And the quick-darting eye of restless Fear,
While cold Oblivion, 'mid thy ruins laid,
Folds his dank wing beneath the ivy shade.

HYMN OF THE CAPTIVE JEWS.

God of the thunder! from whose cloudy seat
　　The fiery winds of desolation flow:
Father of vengeance! that with purple feet,
　　Like a full wine-press treadst the world below:
The embattled armies wait thy sign to slay,
Nor springs the beast of havoc on his prey,
Nor withering Famine walks his blasted way,
　　Till Thou the guilty land hast sealed for woe.

God of the rainbow! at whose gracious sign
　　The billows of the proud their rage suppress;
Father of mercies! at one word of Thine
　　An Eden blooms in the waste wilderness!
And fountains sparkle in the arid sands,
And timbrels ring in maiden's glancing hands,
And marble cities crown the laughing lands,
　　And pillared temples rise Thy name to bless.

O'er Judah's land Thy thunders broke, O Lord!
　　The chariots rattled o'er her sunken gate,
Her sons were wasted by the Assyrian sword,
　　E'en her foes wept to see her fallen state:
And heaps her ivory palaces became,
Her princes wore the captive's garb of shame,
Her temple sank amid the smouldering flame,
　　For Thou didst ride the tempest-cloud of fate.

O'er Judah's land Thy rainbow, Lord, shall beam,
　　And the sad city lift her crownless head;
And songs shall wake, and dancing footsteps gleam,
　　Where broods o'er fallen streets the silence of the dead.
The sun shall shine on Salem's gilded towers,
On Carmel's side our maidens cull the flowers,
To deck, at blushing eve, their bridal bowers,
　　And angel-feet the glittering Sion tread.

Thy vengeance gave us to the stranger's hand,
　　And Abraham's children were led forth for slaves;
With fettered steps we left our pleasant land,
　　Envying our fathers in their peaceful graves.
The stranger's bread with bitter tears we steep,
And when our weary eyes should sink to sleep,
'Neath the mute midnight we steal forth to weep,
　　Where the pale willows shade Euphrates' waves.

The born in sorrow shall bring forth in joy;
　　Thy mercy, Lord, shall lead Thy children home;

He that went forth a tender yearling boy,
 Yet, ere he die, to Salem's streets shall come.
And Canaan's vines for us their fruits shall bear,
And Hermon's bees their honeyed stores prepare ;
And we shall kneel again in thankful prayer,
   Where, o'er the cherub-seated God, full blazed the
      irradiate dome.

OH ! WEEP FOR THOSE.

Oh ! weep for those that wept by Babel's stream,
Whose shrines are desolate, whose land a dream ;
Weep for the harp of Judah's broken shell ;
Mourn—where their God hath dwelt, the godless dwell !

And where shall Israel lave her bleeding feet ?
And when shall Zion's songs again seem sweet ?
And Judah's melody once more rejoice
The hearts that leap'd before its heavenly voice ?

Tribes of the wandering foot and weary breast,
How shall ye flee away and be at rest !
The wild-dove hath her nest, the fox his cave,
Mankind their country—Israel but the grave !

ON JORDAN'S BANKS.

On Jordan's banks the Arab's camels stray,
On Sion's hill the False One's votaries pray,
The Baal-adorer bows on Sinai's steep—
Yet there—even there—O God ! Thy thunders sleep

There—where Thy finger scorch'd the tablet stone !
There—where Thy shadow to Thy people shone !
Thy glory shrouded in its garb of fire :
Thyself—none living see and not expire !

Oh ! in the lightning let Thy glance appear ;
Sweep from his shiver'd hand the oppressor's spear :
How long by tyrants shall Thy land be trod ?
How long Thy temple worshipless, O God !

HYMN OF THE HEBREW MAID.

When Israel, of the Lord beloved,
   Out from the land of bondage came,
Her father's God before her moved,
   An awful guide in smoke and flame.
By day along the astonish'd lands
   The cloudy pillar glided slow ;
By night Arabia's crimson'd sands
   Return'd the fiery pillar's glow.

There rose the choral hymn of praise,
   And trump and timbrel answered keen ;
And Zion's daughters poured their lays,
   With priest's and warrior's voice between.
No portents now our foes amaze,
   Forsaken Israel wanders lone ;
Our fathers would not know Thy ways,
   And Thou hast left them to their own.

But present still, though now unseen,
   When brightly shines the prosperous day,
Be thoughts of Thee a cloudy screen
   To temper the deceitful ray.
And oh! when stoops on Judah's path
   In shade and storm the frequent night,
Be Thou long suff"ring, slow to wrath,
   A burning and a shining light :

Our harps we left by Babel's streams,
   The tyrants' jest, the Gentiles' scorn.
No censer round our altar beams,
   And mute are timbrel, trump, and horn :
But Thou hast said,—"The blood of goat,
   The flesh of rams I will not prize ;
A contrite heart, an humble thought,
   Are mine accepted sacrifice."

"BY THE WATERS OF BABYLON."

The sun flashed on the royal domes
   Of Babylon the great—
The captives sat upon the stones
   Without the water gate ;

The river through the willows rushed,
    Where they their harps hath hung,
For sorrow all their songs had hushed
    And all their harps unstrung.

Forth came a thoughtless city throng,
    And round the mourners drew—
"Come, sing to us a Sion song,
    And string your harps anew."
" Ah no, not so!" the captives said,
    " Not in a stranger land :
Song from our hearts is banishèd,
    And skill from every hand."

"Jerusalem! dear Jerusalem,
    Could thy sons sing or play,
And thou that art all earth to them
    So fallen and far away ?
Oh, Sion! may the tongue or hand,
    That first forgets thee, rot—
If thou art fallen, dear native land,
    Thou art not quite forgot."

The Babylonian troop are gone,
    In thoughtful mood, away—
The rivers and their tears flow on,
    And none their grief gainsay ;
Their sad harps on the willows swing,
    Their lips in secret pray—
That yet in Sion they may sing,
    Their native Sion lay.

ARIEL.

ARIEL! Ariel! City of our God,
How art thou fallen! no more the voice of prayer
Ascends from thy proud temple ; nor repair
The tribes of Judah, o'er the sacred sod,
To worship where their fathers' feet have trod.
How long, oh God, how long wilt Thou forbear ?
How long the oppressor of Thy people spare ?
How long must Israel bow beneath Thy rod ?
Thou hast, O Lord, from Egypt brought a vine,
Preparèd room, and planted it. The land
Was cover'd with its shadow, oh, return,
Revisit it, and cause Thy face to shine ;
And place upon Thy servant Thy right hand;
So we to call upon Thy name shall learn.

NEHEMIAH.

O TRUE light heart!
Light as the dancing bubbles of red wine
That crown the cup for him, almost divine,
    Whose cup-bearer thou art.

Why art thou sad?
Kings with great cares like not sour looks, and thou
Wast chosen for thy ever-sparkling brow,
    And smile aye sunny-glad.

Thou art not sick;
Sullen thou never wert; as free thy song,
Though captive, as a bird's the meads among
    And copses thick.

Light heart, but true!
True to thy God 'mid Shushan's golden dream,
True to those hearts that wept by Babel's stream,
    Thou'rt still a Jew.

To-day thine eye
Sees not the sparkling wine, the gilded hall;
But, far beside a city's broken wall,
    A tomb dishonoured, lie.

True heart, again be light!
Thy God hath heard thee, and the king hath said,
"Go, build the wall that guards the sacred dead—
    Go, in my might."

Go, guileless Nehemiah,
Serpent Sanballat lurks beside the wall,
And, low among the stones, with scorpion crawl,
    The slave Tobiah.

But fear them not!
Nor yet the craven crew within, their prey,
False prophets, mongrel priests, cheats, usurers grey.
    How changed thy lot!

True heart, but light no more!
The world's rude breath hath blown the froth away
That hid the clear dark wine; O Tirshatha,
    Thy happiest days are o'er!

So from the heavenly throne
Good angels sent to comfort them that mourn

Are never seen to smile till they return,
  And hear their Lord's "Well done."

Stout heart, clear head, clean hand,
An upward eye that sees the guiding light;
These shall direct thy way through darkest night
  Unto the far bright land.

All slept beneath the moon
That night, when thou didst thread thy lonely way
Along the hallowed boundary, where lay
  In heaps the wall o'erthrown.

But lo! the rubbish stirs!
The heaps revive beneath the busy hands
Of soldier-masons, wielding tools, or brands,
  As sound the trumpeters.

Stone treads on stone,
With solemn march moves on the wall divine,
'Mid taunting foes, along the broken line
  That once was Sion's zone.

And soon the ends shall meet!
And clasp again a virgin undefiled,
And thou shalt bring her, cleansed and reconciled,
  To her Redeemer's feet.

The Lord remember thee?
Yes; nought thou ever didst for Him give up,
Heart's lightness, peace, or pleasure's sparkling cup,
  But shall remembered be.

To thee it shall be given,
To shine among the saints at Christ's right hand,
With Moses and Elias there to stand,
  And crown the cup of heaven.

THE MESSIAH.

A great part of this poem is taken from Isaiah's prophetic description of Christ's kingdom.

YE nymphs of Solyma! begin the song :
To heavenly themes sublimer strains belong.
The mossy fountains and the sylvan shades,
The dreams of Pindus and th' Aonian maids,
Delight no more. O Thou my voice inspire,
Who touched Isaiah's hallowed lips with fire!

Rapt into future times the bard begun !
A virgin shall conceive, a virgin bear a son !
From Jesse's root behold a Branch arise,
Whose sacred flower with fragrance fills the skies :
Th' ethereal Spirit o'er its leaves shall move,
And on its tops descend the mystic Dove.
Ye heavens ! from high the dewy nectar pour,
And in soft silence shed the kindly shower ;
The sick and weak, the healing plant shall aid,
From storms a shelter, and from heat a shade.
All crimes shall cease, and ancient frauds shall fail ;
Returning Justice lift aloft her scale ;
Peace o'er the world her olive-wand extend,
And white-robed Innocence from heaven descend.
Swift fly the years, and rise th' expected morn !
O spring to light ! auspicious Babe, be born !
See, Nature hastes her earliest wreaths to bring
With all the incense of the breathing spring :
See lofty Lebanon his head advance :
See nodding forests on the mountain dance.
See spicy clouds from lowly Sharon rise,
And Carmel's flowery top perfume the skies !
Hark ! a glad voice the lonely desert cheers.
Prepare the way ! a God, a God appears :
A God, a God ! the vocal hills reply :
The rocks proclaim th' approaching Deity.
Lo, earth receives Him from the bending skies :
Sink down, ye mountains : and ye valleys, rise :
With heads declined, ye cedars, homage pay :
Be smooth, ye rocks, ye rapid floods, give way !
The Saviour comes, by ancient bards foretold !
Hear him, ye deaf ; and all ye blind, behold !
He from thick films shall purge the visual ray,
And on the sightless eyeball pour the day ;
'Tis He the obstructed paths of sound shall clear,
And bid new music charm the unfolding ear :
The dumb shall sing, the lame his crutch forego,
And leap exulting like the bounding roe.
No sigh, no murmur, the wide world shall hear ;
From every face He wipes off every tear.
In adamantine chains shall death be bound,
And hell's grim tyrant feel the eternal wound.
As the good shepherd tends his fleecy care,
Seeks freshest pasture and the purest air ;
Explores the lost, the wandering sheep directs ;
By day o'ersees them, and by night protects ;
The tender lambs he raises in his arms,
Feeds from his hands, and in his bosom warms ;
Thus shall mankind His guardian care engage,—
The promised Father of the future age.
No more shall nation against nation rise,

Nor ardent warriors meet with hateful eyes,
Nor fields with gleaming steel be covered o'er,
The brazen trumpets kindle rage no more :
But useless lances into scythes shall bend,
And the broad falchion in a ploughshare end :
Then palaces shall rise ; the joyful son
Shall finish what his short-lived sire begun ;
Their vines a shadow to their race shall yield,
And the same hand that sowed shall reap the field ;
The swain in barren deserts with surprise
Sees lilies spring, and sudden verdure rise ;
And starts, amidst the thirsty wilds, to hear
New falls of water murmuring in his ear.
On rifted rocks, the dragon's late abodes,
The green reed trembles, and the bulrush nods.
Waste, sandy valleys, once perplexed with thorn,
The spiry fir and stately box adorn ;
To leafless shrubs the flowery palms succeed,
And odorous myrtle to the noisome weed :
The lambs with wolves shall graze the verdant mead,
And boys in flowery bands the tiger lead :
The steer and lion at one crib shall meet,
And harmless serpents lick the pilgrim's feet.
The smiling infant in his hand shall take
The crested basilisk and speckled snake ;
Pleased, the green lustre of the scales survey,
And with their forkèd tongue shall innocently play.
 Rise, crowned with light, imperial Salem, rise !
Exalt thy towery head, and lift thy eyes !
See a long race thy spacious courts adorn ;
See future sons and daughters yet unborn,
In crowding ranks on every side arise,
Demanding life, impatient for the skies :
See barbarous nations at thy gates attend,
Walk in thy light, and in thy temple bend :
See thy bright altars thronged with prostrate kings,
And heaped with products of Sabæan springs.
For thee Idumè's spicy forests blow,
And seeds of gold in Ophir's mountains glow.
See heaven its sparkling portals wide display,
And break upon thee in a flood of day !
No more the rising sun shall gild the morn,
Nor evening Cynthia fill her silver horn,
But lost, dissolved in thy superior rays,
One tide of glory, one unclouded blaze,
O'erflow thy courts : the Light Himself shall shine
Revealed, and God's eternal day be thine !
The seas shall waste, the skies in smoke decay,
Rocks fall to dust, and mountains melt away :
But fixed His word, His saving power remains :
Thy realm for ever lasts, thy own Messiah reigns.

THE REPENTANCE OF NINEVEH.

An ancient city once with all its towers,
Its domes, its turrets, bath'd in golden hours,
   Lay basking on the plain.
From balcony and window went a voice
Of music sweet, and cry, "Rejoice, rejoice,
   "And dance and feast, and feast and dance again."

In luxury, and pomp, and love, and flowers,
In garlands, garments gay, and perfum'd showers
   Each day and night did wane.
And still with wine, and song, and dulcet noise
Did sackbut, harp and lute exhort "rejoice
   And feast and dance, and dance and feast again."

But hark! A voice above the revels ringing,
Like bells at midnight by an earthquake swinging:
   "Destruction comes! repent.
Yet forty days this place shall be overthrown,
Fire and whirlwind rend it stone from stone,
   Madmen! repent! repent!"

And thro' the festive streets a being spectral,
Like one by fiends pursued, with voice sepulchral,
   Who ran and cried "Repent
From Hell's red depths beneath the ocean's gloom,
Where Death's black weeds enwrap'd me for my doom,
   Back to the world I'm sent,
To summon you when forty days expire,
To shoreless seas of brimstone and of fire.
   Repent! repent! repent!"
With haggard face, and eyes dilated staring,
Gigantic form and wan, with wild locks flaring,
He paused not, turned not, like a meteor flying,
Till in the distance as the spent storm dying,
   Was heard "repent! repent!"

Then ceas'd the music, harp and dulcimer,
And dancing feet no longer gleaming were:
   All lips turned pale.
Goblets o'erthrown, silent the riot bout,
The idol's song, the wine-inspired shout,
   Chang'd to one wail.

Till the King with love-kissed garland crown'd,
Snapp'd ev'ry jewel'd knot and cast it on the ground:
   "One hope! to prayer, to prayer!
"The God of Heaven may yet withstay His hand,
If humble fasting, weeping, all the land
   Cry mightily to spare."

  *   *   *   *   *   *   *   *

Yes! God beheld repentant man with pity.
A day of grace He gave that humbl'd city,
    A mis-spent day of grace.
Ah Nineveh! amid thy ruins lone
Sits devastation on thy threshold stone
    And stares into thy face

Amid thy cedar-courts are wild beasts lying,
And on thy broken walls the dry grass sighing
    To days gone by.
While in thy lintels, whence sweet lutes did swell,
Now cormorants lodge and shriek and bitterns dwell.
    With their discordant cry.

   *   *   *   *   *   *   *

Oh let us read the past with introspection,
As illustrating the Divine reflection,
    In warning given,
That they who slight the Prophets and the Law
Not long repent altho' the dead they saw
    Beckon to Heaven.

And in these forty days " bewailing wholly
With all contrition and with meekness" lowly
    Our sinfulness of yore.
So shall be thus " the day of vengeance wrathful,
And voice of most just judgment" awful
    Averted from our shore.

BABYLON IS FALLEN.

FALLEN is stately Babylon !
Her mansions from the earth are gone,
For ever quenched, no more her beam
Shall gem Euphrates' voiceless stream.
Her mirth is hushed, her music fled—
All, save her very name, is dead ;
And the lone river rolls his flood,
Where once a thousand temples stood.

Queen of the golden East ! afar
Thou shonest, Assyria's morning star !
Till God, by righteous anger driven,
Expelled thee from thy place in Heaven.
For false and treacherous was thy ray,
Like swampy lights that lead astray :
And o'er the splendour of thy name
Rolled many a cloud of sin and shame.

For ever fled thy princely shrines,
Rich with their wreaths of clustering vines;
Priest, censer, incense—all are gone
From the deserted altar-stone.
Belshazzar's halls are desolate,
And vanished their imperial state;
Even as the pageant of a dream
That floats unheard on Memory's stream.

Fallen is Babylon! and o'er
The silence of her hidden shore,
Where the gaunt satyr shrieks and sings,
Hath Mystery waved his awful wings.
Concealed from eyes of mortal men,
Or angels' more pervading ken,
The ruined city lies—unknown
Her site to all, but God alone.

THE CITIES OF OLD.

WHERE are the cities which of old in mighty grandeur rose?
Amid the desert's burning sands, or girt with frozen snows;
Is there no vestige now remains, their wond'rous tale to tell,
Of how they blazed like meteor-stars, and how, like them, they fell?

Hark! hark! the voice of prophecy comes o'er the desert wide,
Come down, come down, and in the dust thy virgin beauties hide,
Oh, "Daughter of Chaldea," thou no more enthroned shalt be,
For the desert and the wilderness alone shall tell of thee.

Though old Euphrates still rolls on his everlasting stream,
Thy brazen gates and golden halls are as they ne'er had been,
Where stood thy massy tower-crowned walls, and palaces of pride,
The dragon and the wild beast now therein securely hide.

The "besom of destruction" o'er thee hath swept its way
In wrath, because thine impious hand on God's Anointed lay:
Thou "Lady of the Kingdoms," Chaldea's daughter proud,
Thy gold is dim, thy music mute, and darkness now thy shroud.

Lament, ye seas, and howl, ye isles, for Tyre's virgin daughter,
Who sits a queen enthroned upon the wide far-flowing water,
Who said, "I am above all else with perfect beauty crowned,
And helm and shield in comeliness hang on my walls around;

"My merchant-princes bear the wealth of every land and
  clime,
The choicest things that earth can give, in sea, or air, are
  mine,
The vestments rich of purple dye, alone are made by me,
And kings that robe can only wear, the robe of sovereignty."

And haughty Zidon, she too stood enrobed in dazzling light,
The precious stone her covering was, with pearl and diamond
  bright ;
The ruby and the emerald, the sapphire's glowing gem,
Blazed on her star-embroider'd vest, and on her diadem.

Thou "City of a hundred gates," through whose folding leaves
  of brass,
Ten thousand men in arm'd array, from each at once might
  pass,
Could not thy warriors and thy walls thee from the spoilers
  save ?
Alas ! alas ! thy gates are down, thy heroes in the grave.

And where those sumptuous summer-homes, those bowers of
  kingly pride,
That rose amid the "palm-tree shade," far in the desert wide ?
Where that gigantic structure, the temple of the sun ?
Is thy day of beauty too gone by, thy race of glory run ?

Imperial "Mistress of the World," where are thy triumphs
  now ?
For dark, and dim, and lustreless, are the jewels on thy brow ;
The proud stream at thy feet rolls on, as it was wont of old,
And bears within its azure depths what time may not unfold.

The seven hills thy ancient throne, the hand of time defy,
But now the marble coronets in broken fragments lie,
The stately arch, the pillar'd dome, the palace and the hall,
No more behold in banner'd pride, the gorgeous festival,

Thy Cæsars, and thy citizens, the emperor, and slave,
Alike rest in the silent tomb, or in the silent grave ;
Even there thy noble ladies, in deeds of virtue bold,
And there is Massalina now, in her robe of woven gold.

And thou, beloved Jerusalem, tho' desolate thou art,
Thy honoured name enshrined shall be in every Christian's
  heart,
Tho' the harp of Jesse's son now lies neglected, mute, and still,
Yet Abraham's God cannot forget His own most holy hill.

The silver trumpet yet shall wake in thee a joyous sound,
Thy golden altars be once more with sweetest incense crown'd ;

Yet not the blood of bulls or goats that shall be offered there,
But the sweet incense of the heart, in notes of praise and
    prayer.

The seven-branch lustre yet shall shed its rays of holy light,
On every clustered capital, with sculptured traceries bright,
And He whose presence dwelt between the cherubims of gold,
Shall to His bright pavilion come, as He was wont of old.

For Israel's King of David's line, the Crowned, the Crucified,
Who languished in Gethsemane and who on Calv'ry died,
Yes, He shall come, and gather in of every clime and hue,
Barbarian, Scythian, Indian, Greek ; the Gentile and the Jew.

No light of sun or moon shall then again be needed there,
Nor cooling fountains cast their floods into the balmy air,
But He who is the light and life, in the temple-throne shall
    dwell,
His brightest crown Salvation is, his name Immanuel.

And down the streets of purest gold, bright as transparent
    glass,
Diffusing health and happiness o'er nations as they pass,
The everlasting streams of life their healing waters pour,
And he who tastes those crystal floods, shall faint with thirst
    no more !

TYRE.

In thought, I saw the palace domes of Tyre;
    The gorgeous treasures of her merchandise;
And her proud people in their brave attire,
    Thronging her streets for sport or sacrifice.
I saw the precious stones and spiceries,
The singing girl with flower-wreathed instrument ;
    And slaves whose beauty asked a monarch's price—
Forth from all lands all nations to her went,
And kings to her in embassy were sent.
    I saw, with gilded prow and silken sail,
Her ships that of the sea had government :
    O gallant ships ! 'gainst you what might prevail?
She stood upon her rock, and in her pride
Of strength and beauty, waste and woe defied.

I looked again—I saw a lonely shore,
    A rock amid the waters, and a waste
Of trackless sand ;—I heard the black seas roar,

And winds that rose and fell with gusty haste.
There was one scathèd tree, by storm defaced,
Round which the sea-birds wheeled with screaming cry.
Ere long came on a traveller, slowly paced ;
Now east, then west, he turned with curious eye,
Like one perplexed with an uncertainty.
Awhile he looked upon the sea, and then
Upon a book, as if it might supply
The things he lacked :—he read, and gazed again ;
Yet, as if unbelief so on him wrought,
He might not deem this shore the shore he sought.

Again I saw him come ;—'twas eventide ;—
The sun shone on the rock amidst the sea ;
The winds were hushed ; the quiet billows sighed
With a low swell ; the birds winged silently
Their evening flight around the scathèd tree :
The fisher safely put into the bay,
And pushed his boat ashore ;—then gathered he
His nets, and, hastening up the rocky way,
Spread them to catch the sun's warm evening ray.
I saw that stranger's eye gaze on the scene :
"And this was Tyre!" said he, "how has decay
Within her palaces a despot been !
Ruin and silence in her courts are met,
And on her city rock the fisher spreads his net!"

THE FALL OF NINEVEH.

The days of old return ;—I breathe the air
Of the young world ; I see her giant sons,
Like to a gorgeous pageant in the sky
Of summer's evening, cloud on fiery cloud
Thronging upheaved,—before me rise the walls
Of the Titanic city,—brazen gates,—
Towers,—temples,—palaces enormous piled,—
Imperial NINEVEH, the earthly queen!
In all her golden pomp I see her now,—
Her swarming streets,—her splendid festivals,—
Her sprightly damsels to the timbrel's sound
Airily bounding, and their ankles chime,—
Her lusty sons, like summer-morning gay,—
Her warriors stern,—her rich-robed rulers grave ;
I see her halls sunbright at midnight shine,—
I hear the music of her banquetings ;
I hear the laugh, the whisper, and the sigh.

A sound of stately treading towards me comes,—
A silken wafting on the cedar-floor :
As from Arabia's flowering groves, an air
Delicious breathes around,—tall, lofty-browed,—
Pale and majestically beautiful,—
In vesture gorgeous as the clouds of morn,—
With slow, proud step, her glorious dames sweep by.

Again I look,—and lo ! around the walls
Unnumbered hosts in flaming panoply,—
Chariots like fire, and thunder-bearing steeds !
I hear the shouts of battle : like the waves
Of the tumultuous sea they roll and rush !—
In flame and smoke the imperial city sinks !
Her walls are gone, her palaces are dust—
The desert is around her, and within
Like shadows have the mighty passed away.
Whence, and how came the ruin ? by the hand
Of the oppressor were the nations bowed ;
They rose against him, and prevailed ; for he,
The haughty monarch who the earth could rule,
By his own furious passions was o'er-ruled :
With pride his understanding was made dark,
That he the truth knew not ; and by his lusts,
And by the fierceness of his wrath the hearts
Of men he turned from him. So, to all kings
Be he example. that the tyrannous
And iron rod breaks down at length the hand
That wields it strongest ; that by virtue alone
And justice, monarchs sway the hearts of men ;
For there hath God implanted love of these,
And hatred of oppression, which unseen
And noiseless though it work, yet in the end,
E'en like the viewless elements of the storm,
Brooding in silence, will in thunder burst !
So let the nations learn, that not in wealth,
Nor in the grosser pleasures of the sense,
Nor in the glare of conquest, nor the pomp
Of vassal kings, and tributary lands,
Do happiness and lasting power abide ;—
That virtue unto man best glory is,
His strength, and truest wisdom ;—and that guilt,
Though for a season in the heart delight,
Or to worse deeds the bad man do make strong,—
Brings misery yet, and terror, and remorse,
And weakness and destruction in the end :
So if the nations learn, then not in vain
The mighty one hath been, and is no more !

THE VISION IN THE VALLEY OF DRY BONES.

He walked the vale, where thickly spread,
   And whitening all the ground,
The bones of thousand thousand dead
   Lay scattered all around ;
And like the leaves, all sear and dry,
When autumn's blast hath swept the sky,
   Those bones might there be found ;
And not less thickly were they seen,
Than leaves when autumn's blast hath been.

He stood within that gloomy vale—
   He stood—that hallowed seer ;
A voice was heard upon the gale,
   It sounded in his ear ;
It bade him speak that mighty spell,
Which not e'en powerful death can quell,
   But listens to in fear.
That word of mystic power he spoke—
An awful sound the stillness broke.

Bone linked to bone, with rustling sound,
   As when, through autumn's trees,
The withered leaves fall quickly round
   Upon the mournful breeze ;
And o'er each bone, on that wide plain,
Thus linked, the flesh returned again,—
   Each lay, as if disease
Its all-transforming work had done,
Ere yet corruption has begun.

But still devoid of living breath, .
   Those countless numbers lay ;
Still held within the grasp of death,
   In horrible array :
Their eyes were fixed and glazed,—each brow
Was cold and pale as winter's snow ;
   Each form, but moulded clay ;
Thus silently and grimly spread,
They seem'd a nation of the dead.

Again the heaven-breathed voice was heard—
   Again the seer obeyed—
Again he spoke the mystic word—
   Again its power displayed.
" Come, winds of heaven, and breathe around "—

The winds rushed by with hollow sound—
　And o'er those corses played ;
" Come, winds of heaven, breathe o'er the slain,
That they may wake to life again."

They brooded on those forms—they sped
　Revivifying breath ;—
I saw that mighty host of dead
　Wake from their sleep of death ;
Light danced in every eye—each breast
Began to heave—no more at rest,
　The heart throbbed strong beneath,
The blood flowed warm in every vein,
Life started to its seat again.

BELSHAZZAR.

The king was on his throne,
　The satraps thronged the hall ;
A thousand bright lamps shone
　O'er that high festival.
A thousand cups of gold,
　In Judah deemed divine—
Jehovah's vessels hold
　The godless heathen's wine.

In that same hour and hall
　The fingers of a hand
Came forth against the wall,
　And wrote as if on sand :
The fingers of a man :
　A solitary hand
Along the letters ran,
　And traced them like a wand.

The monarch saw and shook,
　And bade no more rejoice ;
All bloodless waxed his look,
　And tremulous his voice.
" Let the men of lore appear,
　The wisest of the earth,
And expound the words of fear,
　Which mar our royal mirth."

Chaldea's seers are good,
　But here they have no skill ;
And the unknown letters stood

Untold and awful still.
 And Babel's men of age
  Are wise and deep in lore,
 But now they were not sage,
  They saw—but knew no more.

A captive in the land,
 A stranger and a youth,
He heard the king's command,
 He saw that writing's truth.
The lamps around were bright,
 The prophecy in view;
He read it on that night,—
 The morrow proved it true.

" Belshazzar's grave is made,
 His kingdom passed away,
He, in the balance weighed,
 Is light and worthless clay.
The shroud, his robe of state,
 His canopy the stone;
The Mede is at his gate !
 The Persian on his throne !"

BELSHAZZAR'S FEAST.

Joy holds her court in great Belshazzar's hall,
Where his proud lords attend their monarch's call.
The rarest dainties which the teeming East
Pours from her bounteous lap, adorn the feast.
O'er silver fountains perfumed waters play,
And gems add lustre to the blaze of day:
The brightest tears of rich Assyria's vine
In the broad gold with deeper crimson shine:
Mirth dips his pinions in the rosy bowl,
And Music pours his raptures o'er the soul:
While the high domes and fretted roofs prolong
Each dying echo of the choral song.
 But, lo! the Monarch rises.—" Pour," he cries,
" To the great gods, the Assyrian deities;
" Pour forth libations of the rosy wine
" To Nebo, Bel, and all the powers divine.
" Those golden vessels crown, which erewhile stood
" Fast by the oracle of Judah's God ;
" Till that accursèd race provoked the ire
" And vengeful arm of my immortal sire.
" Hail to the Gods, whose omens in the night

"Beamed on my soul through visions of delight."
Ah ! wretched mortal, worthless worm of clay !
Thou grovelling reptile, born but to decay !
The Almighty's wrath shall soon in tempest rise,
And scatter wide thine impious sacrifice,
Roll back the torrent of thy guilty pride,
And whelm thee, boaster, in its refluent tide.
  Such is thine own impending fate, O king !
Else, why that start, that livid cheek ? why fling
The untasted goblet from thy palsied hand ?
Why shake thy joints ? thy feet forget to stand !
Where roams thine eye ? which seems in wild amaze-
To shun some object, yet returns to gaze ;
Then shrinks again appalled, as if the tomb
Had sent a spirit from its inmost gloom,
Dread as the phantom which in night's dark hour
Revealed the terrors of the Almighty's power ;
When o'er the couch of Eliphaz it stood,
And froze the life-streams of his curdling blood.
  Awful the horror, when Belshazzar raised
His arm, and pointed where the vision blazed !
For see ! enrobed in flame, a mystic shade,
As of a hand, a red right-hand, displayed !
And slowly moving o'er the wall, appear
Letters of fate, and characters of fear !
'Tis that Almighty hand, that shakes the pole,
Wings the swift bolt, and bids the thunder roll.
  Breathless they stand in deathlike silence ; all
Fix their glazed eyeballs on the dreaded wall :
It seems as if a magic spell had bound
Each form in icy fetters ; not a sound
Is heard, except some throbbing pulse proclaims
That life still lingers in their sinking frames.
See ! now the vision brightens, now 'tis gone ;
Like meteor flash, like heaven's own lightning flown !
But, though the hand hath vanished, still appear
Those mystic characters of fate and fear ;
Baffling each effort vainly made to scan
Such revelation of the Lord to man.
  " Quick bring the Prophet ;—let his piercing eye
" Scan these dim outlines of futurity :
" And, oh ! in mercy let his tongue proclaim
" The mystery of that visionary flame.'"
The holy prophet came, with brow serene,
With spirit speaking eye, and lofty mien.
To whom Belshazzar :—" Prophet, by thine aid
" Be our sad doubts and anxious cares allayed.
" Our sage Chaldeans now in vain explore
" The secret wonders of their magic lore.
" See the dire portents that our hearts appal;
" Read thou the lines upon that dreaded wall.

" Nor shall thy skill and high deserts forego
" The richest gifts a monarch can bestow."
   Unutterably awful was the eye
Which met the monarch's; and the stern reply
Fell heavy on his soul. "Thy gifts withhold,
" Nor tempt the Spirit of the Lord with gold.
" Did memory fail thee? was thy father's lot
" So lightly noted, and so soon forgot?
" Him God exalted; him the Almighty gave
" Power to cast down, set up, destroy, or save.
" But when the hand that raised him, he defied,
" It smote him, and he withered in his pride;
" An awful wreck of man, outcast of heaven,
" From human haunts, from social converse driven.
" At length relenting heaven his pride subdued,
" Restored his reason, and his form renewed.
" Then humbly bent beneath the hand that shed
" Mercies or judgments on his chastened head,
" The covering shield he blessed, or kissed the rod,
" And bowed submissive to the will of God.
" But thou, unmindful of thy sire's release,
" His pride and fall, his penitence and peace,
" Hast braved the fury of the living Lord,
" Profaned His vessels, and His rites abhorred.
" Proud monarch, hear what these dread words reveal'!
" That lot on which the Eternal sets his seal.
" Thy kingdom numbered, and thy glory flown,
" The Mede and Persian revel on thy throne.
" Weighed in the balance, thou hast kicked the beam;
" See to yon western sun the lances gleam,
" Which, ere his orient rays adorn the sky,
" Thy blood shall sully with a crimson dye."
   This fate foretold, the strains prophetic cease.
But ere the prophet's feet depart in peace,
The chain of gold upon his neck they cast,
The robe of scarlet gird around his waist;
And proclamations through the land declare
Daniel third ruler, next Assyria's heir.
In the dire carnage of that night's dread hour,
Crushed 'mid the ruins of his crumbling power,
Belshazzar fell: though secret was the blow,
Unknown the hand that laid the tyrant low.

DANIEL'S SOLILOQUY.

"And what is death, my friend, that I should fear it?
To die! why 'tis to triumph; 'tis to join
The great assembly of the good and just;
Immortal worthies, heroes, prophets, saints!
Oh! 'tis to join the band of holy men,
Made perfect by their suff'rings! 'Tis to meet
My great progenitors! 'tis to behold
Th'illustrious Patriarchs; they, with whom the Lord
Deign'd hold familiar converse! 'Tis to see
Bless'd Noah and his children, once a world!
'Tis to behold (oh! rapture to conceive!)
Those we have known, and lov'd, and lost, below!
Bold Azariah, and the band of brothers,
Who sought, in bloom of youth, the scorching flames!
Nor is it to behold heroic men
Alone, who fought the fight of faith on earth;
But heav'nly conquerors, angelic hosts,
Michael and his bright legions, who subdued
The foes of Truth! To join their blest employ
Of love and praise! To the high melodies
Of choirs celestial to attune my voice,
Accordant to the golden harps of saints!
To join in bless'd Hosannahs to their King!
Whose face to see, whose glory to behold,
Alone were heav'n, tho' saint or seraph none
There were beside, and only HE were there!
This is to die! Who would not die for this?
Who would not die, that he might live for ever?"

DANIEL'S PROPHECY—THE FALL OF BABYLON.

"An impulse more than human stirs my breast.
Rapt in prophetic vision, I behold
Things hid as yet from mortal sight. I see
The dart of vengeance tremble in the air,
Ere long to pierce the impious king. Ev'n now
The fierce, destroying angel stalks abroad,
And brandishes aloft the two-edg'd sword
Of retribution keen; he soon will strike,
And Babylon shall weep as Sion wept.

Pass but a little while, and you shall see
This queen of cities prostrate on the earth.
This haughty mistress of the kneeling world,
How shall she sit dishonour'd in the dust,
In tarnish'd pomp and solitary woe !
How shall she shroud her glories in the dark,
And in opprobrious silence hide her head !
Lament, O virgin daughter of Chaldea !
For thou shalt fall, imperial queen ! shalt fall !
No more Sidonian robes shall grace thy limbs.
To purple garments, sackcloth shall succeed ;
And sordid dust and ashes shall supply
The od'rous nard and cassia. Thou, who said'st,
I am, and there is none beside me : thou,
Ev'n thou, imperial Babylon ! shalt fall :
Thy glory quite eclips'd ! The pleasant sound
Of viol, and of harp, shall charm no more ;
Nor song of Syrian damsels shall be heard,
Responsive to the lute's luxurious note.
But the loud bittern's cry, the raven's croak,
The bat's fell scream, the lonely owl's dull plaint,
And every hideous bird with ominous shriek,
Shall scare affrighted Silence from thy walls.
While DESOLATION, snatching from the hand
Of Time the scythe of ruin, sits aloft,
In dreadful majesty and horrid pomp ;
Glancing with sullen pride thy crumbling tow'rs,
Thy broken battlements, thy columns fall'n :
Then pointing to the mischiefs she has made,
The fiend exclaims, " This once was Babylon."

THE MACCABEES.

DARKNESS o'ershadows Israel all,
    Woe and death and lamentation ;
The heathen laughs on Sion's wall,
    The Temple all is desolation;
A dumb demoniac shape of stone
    Enthroned upon God's holy altar,
Where children of the Faith kneel down
    And fearful Priests thro' false rites falter.

Buried the Book of God, the spirit
    Of Moses and of David gone—
Lost the traditions they inherit,

Their Sabbath scoffed and spat upon ;
Meek recusants with bent necks bare
  Beseech swift death from fire and sword.
Of all deliverance in despair
  Die, rather than deny their Lord.

But other men of hardier mood,
  In Modin's mountains wandered free,
Their temple the o'erarching wood,
  The cave their solemn sanctuary ;
Men who had sworn they would not die
  Like shamble sheep a willing prey ;
Had sworn to smite the foe though he
  Assailed them on the Sabbath day.

Their Chiefs were Judas—Israel's shield
  Her sword, her staff, her morning star,
The first in every fatal field
  To bear the burden of the war ;
And Simon sage, the man of lore,
  Whose downcast eyes read coming signs;
Whose thoughts were spies, skilled to explore
  Afar the invader's dark designs.

Oh, valiant Assidean Chiefs,
  How well your Father's will ye wrought,
How lifted Israel from her griefs,
  And bore her on your shields aloft ;
" She shall not perish,"—so you swore—
  " They shall not root us out of earth,
Our Fathers' God we dare adore,
  And rule the realm that gave us birth."

Oh noble pair, with awful odds,
  Seron, Lysias, Nicanor, come !
Their trust is in their Syrian gods,
  But Israel's hope is in her Own ;
How valiantly year after year
  Ye gird your loins for warfare grand !
How proud, at last your flag you rear,
  On a regenerated land !

A HEBREW MELODY.

On Carmel's brow the wreathy vine
  Had all its honours shed,
And o'er the vales of Palestine
  A sickly paleness spread;
When the old seer, by vision led,
  And energy sublime,
Into that shadowy region sped,
  To muse on distant time.

He saw the valleys far and wide,
  But sight of joy was none;
He look'd o'er many a mountain side,
  But silence reigned alone,
Save that a boding voice sung on,
  By wave and waterfall,
As still, in harsh and heavy tone,
  Deep unto deep did call.

On Kison's strand and Ephrata
  The hamlets thick did lie;
No wayfarer between he saw,
  No Asherite passed by:
No maiden at her task did ply,
  No sportive child was seen;
The lonely dog barked wearily
  Where dwellers once had been.

Oh! beauteous were the palaces
  On Jordan wont to be,
And still they glimmered to the breeze,
  Like stars beneath the sea!
But vultures held their jubilee
  Where harp and cymbal rung,
And there, as if in mockery,
  The baleful satyr sung.

But who had seen that Prophet's eye
  On Carmel that reclined!
It looked not on the times gone by,
  And those that were behind:
His grey hair streamed upon the wind,
  His hands were raised on high,
As mirror'd on his mystic mind
  Arose futurity.

He saw the feast in Bozrah spread,
   Prepared in ancient day;
Eastward, away the eagle sped,
   And all the birds of prey.
"Who's this," he cried, "comes by the way
   Of Edom, all Divine,
Travelling in splendour, whose array
   Is red, but not with wine?"

Blest be the herald of our King
   That comes to set us free!
The dwellers of the rock shall sing,
   And utter praise to Thee!
Tabor and Hermon yet shall see
   Their glories glow again,
And blossoms spring on field and tree,
   That ever shall remain.

"The happy child in dragon's way
   Shall frolic with delight;
The lamb shall round the leopard play,
   And all in love unite;
The dove on Zion's hill shall light,
   That all the world must see.
Hail to the Journeyer, in His might,
   That comes to set us free!"

WATCHMAN! WHAT OF THE NIGHT?

Watchman! tell us of the night,
   What its signs of promise are:
Traveller! o'er yon mountain's height
   See that glory-beaming star!
Watchman! doth its beauteous ray
   Aught of hope or joy foretell?
Traveller! yes! it brings the day,
   Promis'd day of Israel.

Watchman! tell us of the night;
   Higher yet that star ascends:
Traveller! blessedness and light,
   Peace and truth its course portends.
Watchman! will its beams alone

Gild the spot that gave them birth?
Traveller! ages are its own,
  And it bursts o'er all the earth.

Watchman! tell us of the night,
  For the morning seems to dawn:
Traveller! darkness takes its flight,
  Doubt and terror are whithdrawn.
Watchman! let thy wand'rings cease;
  Hie thee to thy quiet home:
Traveller! lo! the Prince of Peace,
  Lo! the Son of God is come.

THE HARP OF CANAAN.

HISTORICAL INCIDENTS OF THE NEW TESTAMENT.

MESSIAH'S ADVENT.

He came not in his people's day
　Of miracle and might,
When awe-struck nations owned their sway
　And conquest crown'd each fight ;—
When nature's self with wonder saw
Her ancient power, her boasted law,
　To feeble man give way——
The elements of earth and heaven
　Israel stayed—for Judah riven !

Pillar and cloud Jehovah gave,
　High emblems of His grace ;
And clove the rock, and smote the wave,
　Moved mountains from their place ;—
But judgment was with mercy blent—
In thunder was the promise sent—
　Fierce lightning veiled His face ;
The jealous God—the burning law—
Were all the chosen people saw.

Behold them—pilgrim tribes no more—
　The promis'd land their own ;
And blessings theirs of sea and shore ;
　To other realms unknown :
From age to age a favoured line,
Of mighty kings and seers divine,
　A temple and a throne ;
Not then, but in their hour of shame,
　Woe, want, and weakness—then " He came

Not in the earthquake's rending force,
　Not in the blasting fire;
Not in the strong wind's rushing course,

Came He, their soul's desire !
Forerunners of His coming these,
Proclaiming over earth and seas,
   As God, His might and ire :
The still, small voice—the hovering dove,
Proved Him Messiah—spoke Him "Love !"

Of life the way, of light the spring
   Eternal, undefiled :
Redeemer, Prophet, Priest, and King—
   Yet came He as a child !
And Zion's favoured eye grown dim,
Knew not her promised Lord in Him
   The lowly and the mild !
She saw the manger, and the tree,
And scornful cried—" Can this be He !"

ADVENT.

I.

O Saviour, is the promise fled?
   Nor longer might Thy grace endure,
To heal the sick and raise the dead,
   And preach Thy Gospel to the poor?
Come, Jesus, come, return again,
   With brighter beam Thy servants bless,
Who long to feel Thy perfect reign,
   And share Thy kingdom's happiness.
A feeble race, by passion driven,
   In darkness and in doubt we roam,
And lift our anxious eyes to Heaven,
   Our hope, our harbour, and our home.
Yet 'mid the wild and wintry gale.
   When Death rides darkly o'er the sea,
And strength and earthly daring fail,
   Our prayers, Redeemer, rest on Thee.
Come, Jesus, come, and as of yore
   The prophet went to clear Thy way,
A harbinger Thy feet before,
   A dawning to Thy brighter day,
So now may grace with heavenly shower,
   Our stony hearts for truth prepare;
Sow in our souls the seed of power,
   Then come and reap Thy harvest there.

II.

In sun and moon and stars
    Signs and wonders there shall be;
Earth shall quake with inward wars,
    Nations with perplexity.
Soon shall ocean's hoary deep,
    Toss'd with stronger tempests, rise;
Darker storms the mountain sweep,
    Redder lightning rend the skies.
Evil thoughts shall shake the proud,
    Racking doubt and restless fear;
And, amid the thunder cloud,
    Shall the Judge of men appear.
And though from that awful face
    Heaven shall fade and earth shall fly,
Fear not ye, His chosen race,
    Your redemption draweth nigh.

III.

Now gird your patient loins again,
    Your wasting torches trim;
And Chief of all the sons of men,—
    Who will not welcome Him?
Rejoice, the hour is near, at length
    The Journeyer on His way
Comes in the greatness of his strength
    To keep His holy day.
With cheerful hymns and garlands sweet,
    Along His wintry road,
Conduct Him to his green retreat,
    His sheltered, safe abode;
Fill all His courts with sacred songs;
    And from the temple wall
Wave verdure o'er the joyful throngs
    That crowd His festival.
And still more greenly in the mind
    Store up the hopes sublime
Which then were born for all mankind,
    So blessèd was the time;
And underneath those hallowed eaves
    A Saviour will be born
In every heart that Him receives
    On His triumphal morn.

IV.

O haste the rites of that auspicious day,
When white-robed altars wreathed in living green,
Adorn the temples, and, half-hid, half seen,

The priest and people emulously pay
Glad homage, with the festal chants between;
And, aisles and arches echoing back the strain,
The sylvan tapestry around is stirred;
And voices sweeter than the song of bird
Are resonant within the leafy fane.
If, in the fadeless foliage gathered there,
Pale Nature has so bright an offering,
Where all beside is withered, waste, and bare,
What lively tribute should our spirits bring
To beautify, O Lord, Thy holy place of prayer?

SAINT JOHN THE BAPTIST.

A VOICE from the desert comes awful and still,
" The Lord is advancing—prepare ye the way,"
The word of Jehovah He comes to fulfil,
And o'er the dark world pour the splendour of day.

Bring down the proud mountain, though towering to heaven,
And be the lone valley exalted on high;
The rough path and crookèd be made smooth and even,
For Zion! your King, your Redeemer is nigh.

The beams of salvation His progress illume,
The lone dreary wilderness sings of her God;
The rose and the myrtle shall suddenly bloom,
And the olive of peace spread its branches abroad.

A PRELUDE FOR CHRISTMAS.

THE seer—that same Prophet child
Who dwelt in Sennaar undefil'd—
Foretold with fire arointed lips
The elder law's Apocalypse:
How, prone on Tigris shore, he saw
The vision filled with acts of awe—
All Heaven's designs in earthly things
The course of kingdoms and of kings—
Th' Egyptian's, Persian's, Grecian's fate:
But saddest scene! saw Sion's state—
The second temple overthrown
From pinnacle to corner stone—
The eternal sacrifice supprest

By unbelievers from the west,
Dense darkness in Judean skies
Till Michael, Israel's Prince, arise—
And He, the Saint of saints, descend
On earth, captivity to end!

Round rolled the times, and Asia knew
What Daniel saw. Then Rome outgrew
All other bounds. War's last wild roar
Lay hushed on the Cantabrian shore—
The Idol of the two-fold face
Looked on his temple's empty space. *
From the far frontier of the Medes
To where day stalls his weary steeds
All men adored at Cæsar's nod,
And frantic cried—a god! a god!
Then when the day had come, and hour,
Augustus spake the word of power,
And kings and consuls, east and west,
Flew to obey their lord's behest—
"Number the nations who obey
Throughout the world the Roman sway."

Then throng'd to tryst earth's ev'ry tribe
Kindred to kin, from ev'ry side;
O'er seas and Alps lost exiles came,
Rivers reversed—some source to claim:
Ganges to Gadès—floods of men
Thronged fleet and port and foot-marked glen—
The very desert seemed to be
Peopled by Cæsar's dread decree—
"Number the nations who obey
Throughout the world the Roman sway.'

Lo! from their Galilean home
Where two of Cæsar's subjects come!
Like loving sire and daughter, they
Hold reverent converse on their way.
Afoot and simply clad, yet grace
Abundant shines in either face:
He, Heli's son, a serious man,
Whom every sign speaks artisan:
She, fairest of all Israel's fair,
All heavenly goodness in her air,
Conscious of royal David's blood
And of her holy motherhood,
Turns to her guide with filial ear,
Well pleased his reverent speech to hear.

---

* The temple of Janus was shut at Rome in the 40th year of Augustus, the year of our Lord's birth at Bethlehem Judah, and remained shut for the supposed space of twelve years.

December's breath breathes keen and chill
On Jacob's well from Ebal's hill,
The wintry sun looks worn and dim
On Sichem from Mount Gerizim,
As paces slowly from the North
That mother near her baby's birth,
Through ways Samarian, rude and wild,
Borne and not bow'd, by such a child !
For thou Ephrata * art to be
The Man-God's destined nursery !
For Thee alone, the star shall rise !
For Thee alone the morning skies
Shall brighten to the angelic song.
Above the troubled shepherd throng !
For Thee, those Angel-aided seers
By Ader's † tower, shall calm their fears,
And ravished by the heavenly strain,
Shall seek their Lord beyond the plain !
For Thee, the star-led Magi bring,
From the far East their offering !
For Thee, shall guilty Herod quiver,
Ephrata ! blessed be thou for ever !

Draw we the veil—this mystery
Is all too bright for mortal eye ;—
How shall it then by mortal tongue
In earthly strain, be fitly sung ?
In Heaven alone, by His own choir,
Where dwells the glorified Desire,
Can worthily be raised the psalm
That hailed on Earth the dread I AM

THE ANNUNCIATION OF THE BLESSÈD VIRGIN MARY.

Oh ! Thou who deign'st to sympathize
With all our frail and fleshly ties,
  Maker, yet Brother dear,
Forgive the too presumptuous thought
If, calming wayward grief, I sought
  To gaze on Thee too near.

---

* Ephrata; the original (Jebusite) name of Bethlehem.
† *Ader ;* a very ancient Christian tradition pointed to the tower of Ader as the scene of the revelation of Christ's birth to the shepherds, " who were in that country." (St. Luke's Gospel, chap. ii, 8.)

Yet sure 'twas not presumptuous, Lord,
'Twas Thine own comfortable word
   That made the lesson known :
Of all the dearest bonds we prove,
Thou countest sons' and mothers' love
   Most sacred, most Thine own.

When wandering here a little span
Thou took'st on Thee to rescue man,
   Thou hadst no earthly sire ;
That wedded love we prize so dear,
As if our heaven and home were here,
   It lit in Thee no fire.

On no sweet sister's faithful breast
Would'st Thou Thine aching forehead rest.
   On no kind brother lean :
But who—oh perfect filial heart,
E'er did like Thee a true son's part
   Endearing, firm, serene ?

Thou wept'st, meek maiden, mother mild,
Thou wept'st upon thy sinless child,
   Thy very heart was riven :
And yet, what mourning matron here,
Would deem thy sorrows bought too dear
   By all on this side Heaven ?

A Son that never did amiss,
That never shamed His mother's kiss,
   Nor crossed her fondest prayer :
Even from the tree He deigned to bow
For her His agonizèd brow,
   Her, His sole earthly care.

Avé Maria ! Blessed Maid !
Lily of Eden's fragrant shade,
   Who can express the love
That nurtured thee so pure and sweet,
Making thy heart a shelter meet
   For Jesus ? Holy Dove-!

Avé Maria ! Mother blest,
To whom caressing and caressed
   Clings the Eternal Child :
Favoured beyond Archangels' dream,
When first on thee with tenderest gleam
   Thy new-born Saviour smiled.

Blessed is the womb that bear Him—blessed
The bosom where His lips were pressed,
But also blessed are they
Who hear His word and keep it well,
The loving homes where Christ shall dwell,
And never pass away.

HYMN ON THE NATIVITY.

O lovely voices of the sky,
That hymn'd the Saviour's birth!
Are ye not singing still on high,
Ye that sang, "Peace on earth?"
To us yet speak the strains
Wherewith, in days gone by
Ye bless'd the Syrian swains,
O voices of the sky!

O clear and shining light, whose beams,
That hour Heaven's glory shed
Around the palms, and o'er the streams,
And on the Shepherd's head;
Be near, through life and death,
As in that holiest night
Of Hope, and Joy, and Faith,
O clear and shining light!

O star which led to Him, whose love
Brought down man's ransom free;
Where art thou?—'Midst the hosts above,
May we still gaze on thee?-
In heaven thou art not set,
Thy rays earth might not dim—
Send them to guide us yet!
O star which led to Him!

A BETHLEHEM HYMN.

He is come, the Christ of God,-
Left for us His glad abode,
Stooping from His throne of bliss,
To this darksome wilderness.

He has come, the Prince of Peace;
Come to bid our sorrows cease,
Come to scatter with His light,
All the shadows of our night.

He, the Mighty King, has come!
Making this poor earth His home,
Come to bear our sins' sad load;
Son of David, Son of God.

He has come, whose name of grace
Speaks deliverance to our race,
Left for us His glad abode,
Son of Mary, Son of God.

Unto us a Child is born!
Ne'er has earth beheld a morn
Among all the morns of time,
Half so glorious in its prime.

Unto us a Son is given!
He has come from God's own heaven;
Bringing with Him from above,
Holy peace and holy love.

BETHLEHEM.

What are these etherial strains,
Floating o'er Judea's plains?
Burning spirits throng the sky,
With their lofty minstrelsy!
Hark! they break the midnight trance
With the joyous utterance,
" Glory to God and peace to men,
Christ is born in Bethlehem!"

Quench, ye types, your feeble ray,
Shadows, ye may melt away;
Prophecy, your work is done,
Gospel ages have begun!
Temple! quench your altar fires,
For these radiant angel-choirs,
To a ruined world proclaim,
Christ is born in Bethlehem.

Pillowed is His infant head
On a borrowed manger bed!
He, around whose throne above,
Angels hymned their songs of love,
Now is wrapt by virgin's hands,
In earth's meanest swaddling bands;
Once adored by seraphim,—
Now a Babe of Bethlehem.

Eastern sages from afar,
Guided by a mystic star,
Followed till its lustre mild
Brought them to the Heavenly Child
May each providence to me
Like a guiding meteor be,
Bringing nearer unto Him
Once the Babe of Bethlehem!

CHRIST'S NATIVITY.

When Jordan hushed his waters still,
And silence slept on Zion hill;
When Bethlehem's shepherds thro' the night,
Watched o'er their flocks by starry light;

Hark! from the midnight hills around,
A voice of more than mortal sound,
In distant hallelujahs stole,
Wild murmuring o'er the raptured soul.

Then swift to every startled eye,
New streams of glory light the sky;
Heaven bursts her azure gates to pour
Her spirits to the midnight hour.

On wheels of light, on wings of flame,
The glorious hosts of Zion came;
High heaven with songs of triumph rung,
While thus they struck their harps and sung:

O Zion! lift thy raptured eye,
The long-expected hour is nigh;
The joys of nature rise again,
The Prince of Salem comes to reign.

See, Mercy, from her golden urn,
Pours a rich stream to them that mourn;

Behold, she binds with tender care,
The bleeding bosom of despair.

He comes! to cheer the trembling heart,
Bid Satan and his host depart;
Again the day-star gilds the gloom,
Again the bowers of Eden bloom;

O Zion! lift thy raptured eye,
The long-expected hour is nigh;
The joys of Nature rise again,
The Prince of Salem comes to reign.

A CHRISTMAS CAROL.

It came upon the midnight clear,
   That glorious song of old,
From angels bending near the earth
   To touch their harps of gold:—
"Peace on the earth— good will to men,
   From Heaven's all gracious King"—
The world in solemn stillness lay
   To hear the angels sing.

Still through the cloven skies they come,
   With peaceful wings unfurled,
And still their heavenly music floats
   O'er all the weary world;
Above its sad and lowly plains
   They bend on heavenly wing,
And ever o'er its Babel sounds
   The blessèd angels sing!

Yet with the woes of sin and strife,
   The world has suffered long,
Beneath the angel strain have rolled
   Two thousand years of wrong;
And man, at war with man, hears not
   The love song which they bring,
O! hush the noise, ye men of strife,
   And hear the angels sing!

And ye, beneath life's crushing road,
   Whose forms are bending low,
Who toil along the climbing way
   With painful steps and slow;

Look now! for glad and golden hours
   Come swiftly on the wing—
O! rest beside the weary road,
   And hear the angels sing!

For lo, the days are hastening on
   By prophet bards foretold,
When with the ever-circling years
   Comes round the age of gold;
When peace shall over all the earth
   Its ancient splendour fling,
And the whole world send back the song
   Which now the angels sing!

CAROL.

Not in halls of regal splendour,
   Not to princes of the earth,
Did the herald angels render
   Tidings of their monarch's birth;
Not to statesmen, priest or sage,
They proclaimed the golden age,
'Twas the poor man's heritage—
   For on shepherds lowly
   Burst the anthem holy:
     In excelsis gloria,
     Et in terra pax!

Not by worldly wealth or wisdom,
   Not by power of law or sword,
But by service to win freedom,
   And by sorrow, bliss afford—
Born to poverty and pain,
Born to die and thus to reign,
Rescuing man from Satan's chain—
   Jesus now rules o'er us,
   Swell the joyful chorus!
     In excelsis gloria,
     Et in terra pax!

Glory be to God in heaven,
   Peace on earth, good-will to men!
In the highest, praise be given!
   Angels! strike your harps again!
Justice has on Mercy smiled,
God and men are reconciled

Through Emmanuel new-born child.
  Blend we then our voices,
  Earth with heaven rejoices,
    In excelsis gloria,
    Et in terra pax!

Bid the new-born Monarch welcome,
  Pay Him homage every heart!
Hallelujah! let His kingdom
  Swiftly spread in every part:
War and bloodshed then shall cease,
Selfishness its slaves release,
Love shall reign, and white-robed Peace;
  Then from earth as heaven,
  Praise shall aye be given—
    In excelsis gloria,
    Et in terra pax!

CHRISTMAS.

Christians, awake! salute the happy morn,
Whereon the Saviour of mankind was born;
Rise to adore the mystery of love,
Which hosts of Angels chanted from above:
With them the joyful tidings first begun,
Of God Incarnate, and the Virgin's Son.

Then to the watchful shepherds it was told
Who heard the angelic herald's voice, "Behold,
I bring good tidings of a Saviour's birth,
To you, and all the nations upon earth;
This day hath God fulfill'd His promised word,
This day is born a Saviour, Christ the Lord."

He spake; and straightway the celestial choir
In hymns of joy, unknown before, conspire;
The praises of redeeming love they sang.
And heaven's whole orb with hallelujah rang;
God's highest glory was their anthem still,
Peace upon earth, and unto men good-will.

To Bethlehem straight the enlighten'd shepherds ran,
To see the wonders God had wrought for man;
Then to their flocks, still praising God, return,
And their glad hearts within their bosoms burn;
To all, the joyful tidings they proclaim;
The first Apostles of the Saviour's fame.

Oh! may we keep and ponder in our mind
God's wondrous love in saving lost mankind;
Trace we the Babe, who hath retrieved our loss,
From the poor manger to the bitter cross;
Tread in His steps, assisted by His grace,
Till man's first heavenly state again takes place.

Then may we hope, the angelic hosts among,
To join, redeem'd, a glad triumphant throng;
He that was born upon this joyful day,
Around us all His glory shall display :
Saved by His love, incessant we shall sing
Eternal praise to heaven's Almighty King.

ADESTÈ FIDELES

O COME, all ye faithful,
Joyfully triumphant;
O come ye, O come ye, to Bethlehem;
Come and behold Him,
Born the King of Angels:
O come, let us adore Him,
O come, let us adore Him,
O come, let us adore Him, Christ the Lord.

God of God,
Light of Light,
Lo! He abhors not the Virgin's womb;
Very God,
Begotten, not created;
O come, let us adore Him,
O come, let us adore Him,
O come, let us adore Him, Christ the Lord.

Sing, choirs of Angels,
Sing in exultation,
Sing, all ye powers of heaven above;
Glory to God
In the highest,
O come, let us adore Him,
O come, let us adore Him,
O come, let us adore Him, Christ the Lord.

Yea, Lord, we greet Thee,
Born this happy morning,
JESU, to Thee be glory given;

Word of the Father,
Now in flesh appearing;
O come, let us adore Him,
O come, let us adore Him,
O come, let us adore Him, Christ the Lord.

THE INCARNATION.

For Thou wast born of woman, Thou didst come,
O Holiest! to this world of sin and gloom,
Not in Thy dread omnipotent array;
    And not by thunders strew'd,
    Was Thy tempestuous road;
Nor indignation burned before Thee on Thy way.
    But Thee a soft and naked Child,
    Thy Mother undefiled,
    In the rude manger laid to rest
    From off her virgin breast.

The heavens were not commanded to prepare
A gorgeous canopy of golden air;
Nor stoop'd their lamps th' enthroned fires on high
    A single silent star
    Came wandering from afar,
Gliding uncheck'd and calm along the liquid sky;
    The eastern sages leading on,
    As at a kingly throne,
    To lay their gold and odours sweet
    Before Thy infant feet.

The earth and ocean were not hush'd to hear
Bright harmony from ev'ry starry sphere;
Nor at Thy presence brake the voice of song;
    From all the cherub choirs,
    And seraph's burning lyres,
Pour'd through the host of heaven the charmed cloud along;
    One angel troop the strain began,
    Of all the race of man,
    By simple shepherds heard alone,
    That soft hosanna's tone.

CHRISTMAS DAY.

WHAT sudden blaze of song
　　Spreads o'er th' expanse of heaven?
In waves of light it thrills along,
　　Th' angelic signal given —
"Glory to God!" from yonder central fire
Flows out the echoing lay beyond the starry choir;

　　Like circles widening round
　　　　Upon a clear blue river,
　　Orb after orb, the wondrous sound
　　　　Is echoed on for ever:
"Glory to God on high, on earth be peace,
"And love towards men of love — salvation and release."

　　Yet stay, before thou dare
　　　　To join that festal throng;
　　Listen and mark what gentle air
　　　　First stirr'd the tide of song;
'Tis not; " the Saviour born in David's home,
"To Whom for power and health obedient worlds should come."

　　'Tis not; "the Christ the Lord:"—
　　　　With fix'd adoring look
　　The choir of Angels caught the word,
　　　　Nor yet their silence broke:
But when they heard the sign, where Christ should be,
In sudden light they shone and heavenly harmony.

　　Wrapp'd in His swaddling bands,
　　　　And in His manger laid,
　　The Hope and Glory of all lands
　　　　Is come to the world's aid:
No peaceful home upon His cradle smil'd,
Guests rudely went and came, where slept the royal Child.

　　But where Thou dwellest, Lord,
　　　　No other thought should be,
　　Once duly welcom'd and ador'd,
　　　　How should I part with Thee?
Bethlehem must lose Thee soon, but Thou wilt grace
The single heart to be Thy sure abiding place.

　　Thee, on the bosom laid
　　　　Of a Pure Virgin mind,
　　In quiet ever, and in shade,
　　　　Shepherd and sage may find;
They who have bowed untaught to nature's sway,
And they, who follow Truth along her star-pav'd way.

The pastoral spirits first
  Approach Thee, Babe Divine,
For they in lowly thoughts are mers'd
  Meet for Thy lowly shrine:
Sooner than they should miss where Thou dost dwell,
Angels from Heaven will stoop to guide them to Thy cell.

  Still as the day comes round
    For Thee to be reveal'd,
  By wakeful shepherds Thou art found,
    Abiding in the field
All through the wintry heaven and chill night air,
In music and in light Thou dawnest on their prayer.

  O faint not ye for fear—
    What though your wandering sheep,
  Reckless of what they see and hear,
    Lie lost in wilful sleep?
High Heaven in mercy to your sad annoy,
Still greets you with glad tidings of immortal joy.

  Think on th' eternal home
    The Saviour left for you:
  Think on the Lord most holy, come
    To dwell with hearts untrue:
So shall ye tread untir'd His pastoral ways,
And in the darkness sing your carol of high praise.

THE MADONNA AND CHILD.

  When from Thy beaming throne,
    Oh High and Holy One!
Thou camest to dwell with those of mortal birth,
    No ray of living light
    Flashed on the astonished sight,
To shew the Godhead walked His subject earth.

    Thine was no awful form,—
    Shrouded in mist and storm,—
Of seraph, walking on the viewless wind;
    Nor didst Thou deign to wear
    The port, sublimely fair
Of angel heralds, sent to bless mankind.

    Made like the sons of clay,
    Thy matchless glories lay
8

In form of feeble infancy concealed ;
  No pomp of outward sign
  Proclaimed the Power Divine;
No earthly state the heavenly guest revealed !

  Thou didst not choose Thy home
  Beneath a lordly dome ;
No royal diadem wreathed Thy baby brow;
  Nor on a soft couch laid,
  Nor in rich vest arrayed,
But with the poorest of the poor wert Thou!

  Yet She, whose gentle breast
  Was Thy glad place of rest,
In Her the royal blood of David flowed,
  Men passed her dwelling by
  With proud and scornful eye,
But angels knew and loved her mean abode.

  There softer strains she heard
  Than song of evening bird,
Or tuneful minstrel in a queenly bower;
  And o'er her dwelling lone
  A brighter radiance shone,
Than ever glittered from a monarch's tower.

  For there the mystic star,
  That sages led from far,
To pour their treasures at her Infant's feet,
  Still shed its golden light;
  There, through the calm, clear night,
Were heard angelic voices, strangely sweet.

  Oh happiest Thou of all
  Who bore the deadly thrall,
Which for one mother's crime to all was given;
  Her first of mortal birth
  Brought death to reign on earth,
But *Thine* brings light and life again from heaven!

THE STABLE AT BETHLEHEM.

T'WAS not a palace proud and fair,
He chose for His first home;
No dazz'ling pile of grandeur rare,
With pillar'd hall and dome ; —
Oh no! a stable, humble, poor, —
Received Him at His birth;
And thus was born, unknown, obscure, —
The Lord of Heaven and Earth.

No band of anxious menials there,
To tend the new-born child,
Joseph alone and Mary fair,
Upon the infant smiled;
No broidered linens fine had they
Those little limbs to fold,
No baby garments rich and gay,
No tissues wrought with gold.

Come to your Saviour's lowly bed,
Ye vain and proud of heart!
And learn, with bowed and humbled head,
The lesson 'twill impart; —
'Twill teach ye not to prize too high,
The riches vain of earth, —
But lay up in yon glorious sky
Treasures of truer worth.

And ye, poor stricken sons of grief,
Sad "outcasts" of this life,
Come, too,—ye'll find a sure relief
For your hearts' bitter strife;
Look at Bethlehem's stable poor,
Your Saviour's lowly cot,
Will it not teach ye to endure,
Aye, yes, to bless your lot?

THE EPIPHANY; OR, THE MANIFESTATION OF CHRIST TO THE GENTILES.

BRIGHTEST and Best of the sons of the morning
Dawn on our darkness, and lend us Thine aid!
Star of the East, the horizon adorning,
Guide where our infant Redeemer is laid!

Cold on His cradle the dewdrops are shining!
Low lies His bed with the beasts of the stall!
Angels adore Him in slumber reclining,
Maker, and Monarch, and Saviour of all!

Say shall we yield Him, in costly devotion,
Odours of Edom and offerings divine;
Gems of the mountain, and pearls of the ocean,
Myrrh from the forest, and gold from the mine.

Vainly we offer each ample oblation;
Vainly with gold would His favour secure;

Richer by far is the heart's adoration ;
Dearer to God are the prayers of the poor.

Brightest and Best of the sons of the morning,
Dawn on our darkness, and lend us Thine aid !
Star of the East, the horizon adorning,
Guide where our infant Redeemer is laid !

THE STAR OF BETHLEHEM.

When marshall'd on the nightly plain
    The glittering host bestud the sky ;
One star alone, of all the train,
    Can fix the sinner's wandering eye.

Hark ! hark to God the chorus breaks
    From every host, from every gem ;
But one alone the Saviour speaks—
    It is the Star of Bethlehem.

Once on the raging seas I rode,
    The storm was loud—the night was dark—
The ocean yawn'd—and rudely blow'd
    The wind that toss'd my foundering bark :

Deep horror then my vitals froze ;
    Death-struck, I ceas'd the tide to stem ;
When suddenly a star arose —
    It was the Star of Bethlehem.

It was my guide, my light. my all,
    It bade my dark forebodings cease ;
And thro' the storm and danger's thrall
    It led me to the port of peace.

Now safely moor'd—my perils o'er,
    I'll sing, first in night's diadem,
For ever, and for evermore,
    The star !—the Star of Bethlehem !

THE HOLY INNOCENTS.

Say, ye celestial guards, who wait
In Bethlehem round the Saviour's palace gate,
Say, who are these on golden wings,
That hover o'er the new born King of kings,
Their palms and garlands telling plain
That they are of the glorious martyr train,
Next to yourselves ordained to praise
His name, and brighten as on Him they gaze?

But where their spoils and trophies? where
The glorious dint a martyr's shield should bear?
How chance no cheek among them wears
The deep worn trace of penitential tears,
But all is bright and smiling love,
As if fresh-born from Eden's happy grove,
They had flown here, their king to see,
Nor ever had been theirs of dark mortality.

Ask, and some angel will reply,
" These, like yourselves, were born to sin and die,
But ere the poison root was grown,
God set His seal and mark'd them for his own.
Baptised in blood for Jesus' sake,
Now underneath the Cross-their bed they make,
Nor to be scar'd from that sure rest
By frighten'd mothers' shriek or warrior's waving crest."

Mindful of these, the first-fruits sweet
Borne by the suffering Church her Lord to greet,
Blessed Jesus ever loved to trace
The " innocent brightness " of an infant's face.
He raised them in His Holy arms,
He blessed them from the world and all its harms;
Heirs though they were of sin and shame,
He blessed them in His own and in His father's name.

Then, as each fond unconscious child
On the everlasting Parent sweetly smiled,
(Like infants sporting on the shore,
That tremble not at Ocean's boundless roar.)
Were they not present to Thy thought,
All souls, that in their cradles Thou hast bought?
But chiefly these, who died for Thee
That Thou might'st live for them a sadder death to see

And next to these. Thy gracious word
Was a pledge of benediction, stored

For Christian mothers, while they moan
Their treasured hopes, just born, baptized and gone.
 Oh! joy for Rachel's broken heart!
She and her babes shall meet no more to part;
 So dear to Christ her pious haste
To trust them in His arms, for ever safe embraced.

 She does not grudge to leave them there,
Where to behold them was her heart's first prayer;
 She dares not grieve —but she must weep,
As her pale placid martyr sinks to sleep,
 Teaching so well and silently
How, at the Shepherd's call, the lambs should die,—
 How happier far than life the end
Of souls that infant-like beneath their burthen bend.

RACHEL WEEPING FOR HER CHILDREN.

WEEP, weep not o'er thy children's tomb,
 O Rachel! weep not so:
The bud is cropt by martyrdom,
 The flower in heaven shall blow.

Firstlings of faith! the murderer's knife
 Hath miss'd its deadly aim;
The God, for whom they gave their life,
 For them to suffer came.

Though evil were their days and few,
 Baptized in blood and pain,
He knows them whom they never knew,
 And they shall live again.

Then weep not o'er thy children's tomb,
 O Rachel! weep not so:
The bud is cropt by martyrdom,
 The flower in heaven shall blow.

THE PRESENTATION OF CHRIST IN THE TEMPLE.

Softly the sunbeams gleamed athwart the Temple proud and high,
Built up by Israel's wisest king to the Lord of earth and sky,
Lighting its gorgeous, sculptured roof, and each shining mystic fold
Of the sacred Veil from gaze profane, shielding the Ark of old.

Ne'er had man's boasted art o'er-wrought a scene more rich and bright,
Agate and porphyry—precious gems—cedar and iv'ry white,
Marbles of perfect polish and hue—sculptures and tintings rare,
Costly satin and sandal woods embalming the sacred air.

But see—lo! stealing up yonder aisle, 'mid forest of columns high,
Comes a female form with timid step and downcast modest eye;
A girl—to judge by the fresh young bloom adorning that lovely face,
With locks of gold and vestal brow, and a form of childish grace.

Yet, no, see those soft slight arms close fold a helpless, new-born child,
Late entered on this world of woe—still pure, still undefiled;
Whilst the two white doves she humbly lays before the altar there,
Tell, despite her girlish years, she knows a matron's joy and care.

No fairer sight could heart have asked than that Mother and that Babe,
E'en had He been the child of sin—born to wrath and the grave,
But how must Angelic hosts have looked in breathless rapture on,
Knowing that Child was the Temple's Lord—the Word—th' Eternal Son!

Whilst she was that Virgin Mother pure, fairest of Adam's race—
Whom Heaven's Archangel, bending low, had hailed as full of grace,
Mother of that Saviour God she held, close clasped unto her breast,
That Mary, humble, meek, and poor, whom all ages have called Blessed.

THE PURIFICATION OF THE BLESSÈD VIRGIN.

Bless'd are the pure in heart, for they shall see our God,
The secret of the Lord is theirs, their soul is Christ's abode.

Might mortal thought presume to guess an angel's lay—
Such are the notes that echo through the courts of Heaven to-day.

Such the triumphal hymns on Sion's Prince that wait,
In high procession passing on toward His temple-gate.

Give ear, ye kings—bow down, ye rulers of the earth—
This, this is He; your Priest by grace, your God and King by birth.

No pomp of earthly guards attends with sword and spear,
And all defying, dauntless look, their Monarch's way to clear !

Yet are there more with Him than all that are with you—
The armies of the highest heaven, all righteous, good, and true.

Spotless their robes and pure, dipped in the sea of light
That hides the unapproachèd shrine from men's and angels, sight.

His throne, thy bosom blest, oh Mother undefiled—
That throne, if aught beneath the skies beseems the sinless Child.

Lost in high thoughts " whose son the wondrous Babe might prove,"
Her guiltless husband walks beside, bearing the harmless dove.

Meet emblem of his vow, who, on this happy day,
His dove-like soul—best sacrifice did on God's altar lay.

But who is he, by years, bow'd but erect in heart,
Whose prayers are struggling with his tears ! " Lord, let me now depart ;

" Now hath Thy servant seen Thy saving health, oh Lord :
'Tis time that I depart in peace, according to Thy word."

Yet swells the pomp : once more comes forth to bless her God,
Full fourscore years, meek widow, she her heavenward way hath trod.

She who to earthly joys so long had given farewell,
Now sees unlooked for, Heaven on earth, Christ in His Israel.

Wide open from that hour the temple gates are set,
And still the saints rejoicing there, the Holy Child have met.

Now count His train to-day, and who may meet Him, learn :
Him child-like sires, and maidens find, where pride can nought discern.

Still to the lowly soul He doth Himself impart,
And for His cradle and His throne chooseth the pure in heart.

OUR SAVIOUR'S BOYHOOD.

WITH what a flood of mighty thought,
   Each Christian breast must swell,
When wandering back through ages past,
   Reflection, memory, dwell
On Nazareth's blessed and sacred sod ;
And the boyhood of the Saviour God.

Softly we picture to ourselves,
   That brow serene and fair,
Pure—passionless—the long rich curls.
   Of wavy golden hair ;
And those deep, wond'rous, star-like eyes,
Holy and calm as midnight skies.

We see Him in the work-shop shed,
   With Joseph, wise and good,
Obedient to His guardian's word,
   Docile and meek of mood ;
The mighty Lord of Heaven and Earth,
Toiling like man of lowly birth.

Or else with His young mother fair,
   That sinless, spotless one,
Who watched with such fond, reverent care,
   Her high and glorious Son,
Knowing a matron's joys, griefs, pride,
And yet a Virgin pure beside.

All marvelled at the strange, shy grace
   Of Mary's gentle Son ;
Young mothers envied her the Boy,
   That love from all hearts won ;

And His face watching, sweet and mild,
Asked low of Heaven such a child.

Amid the youth of Nazareth,
  He mingled not in mirth,
And yet all felt most strangely drawn,
  Towards His modest worth;
Despite that quiet, wond'rous Child,
Ne'er laughed, perchance, nor even smiled.

How could He, say! when clearly rose
  Before His spirit's gaze,
The cruel Cross—the griefs, reserved
  His Manhood's future days;
And worse than all, the countless host
That, spite his pangs, would yet be lost.

Silent—reserved—He held His way,
  From morn till evening still,
His thoughts e'er bent on working out
  His mighty Father's will;
Whilst angels bent in ecstacy
'Bove the Boy-God of Galilee.

CHRIST IN THE WILDERNESS.

So saying, he took (for still he knew his power
Not yet expired) and to the wilderness
Brought back the Son of God, and left Him there,
Feigning to disappear. Darkness now rose,
As daylight sunk, and brought in lowering Night,
Her shadowy offspring; unsubstantial both,
Privation mere of light, and absent day.
Our Saviour, meek, and with untroubled mind,
After his aëry jaunt, though hurried sore,
Hungry and cold, betook him to his rest,
Wherever, under some concourse of shades,
Whose branching arms, thick intertwined, might shield
From dews and damps of night His sheltered head:
But, sheltered, slept in vain; for at His head
The tempter watched, and soon with ugly dreams
Disturbed His sleep! And either tropic now
'Gan thunder, and both ends of heaven; the clouds
From many a horrid rift, abortive poured
Fierce rain with lightning mixed, water with fire
In ruin reconciled; nor slept the winds

Within their stony caves, but rushed abroad
From the four hinges of the world, and fell
On the vexed wilderness, whose tallest pines,
Though rooted deep as high, and sturdiest oaks,
Bowed their stiff necks, loaden with stormy blasts,
Or torn up sheer. Ill wast Thou shrouded then,
O patient Son of God, yet only stood'st
Unshaken! Nor yet stay'd the terror there;
Infernal ghosts and hellish furies round
Environed Thee; some howled, some yelled, some shrieked;
Some bent at Thee their fiery darts, while Thou
Sat'st unappalled in calm and sinless peace!
Thus passed the night so foul, till morning fair
Came forth, with pilgrim steps, in amice grey;
Who with her radiant finger stilled the roar
Of thunder, chased the clouds, and laid the winds,
And grisly spectres, which the fiend had raised
To tempt the Son of God with terrors dire.
And now the sun with more effectual beams
Had cheered the face of earth, and dried the wet
From drooping plant, or dropping tree: the birds,
Who all things now behold more fresh and green,
After a night of storm so ruinous,
Cleared up their choicest notes in bush and spray,
To gratulate the sweet return of morn.

THE FASTING.

The Son of God sought with His heavenly Father
    To commune for a space;
Let by the Spirit, He went up from Jordan
    Into a desert place.

What did He meet with in the stony places?
    Did the wild ass draw near?
Did hunted creatures come for His compassion,
    Wild-eyed but void of fear?

Did no bird, wounded, hide herself before Him?
    No lizard dart away?
Did the fox from her hole among the bushes
    Bring out her cubs to play?

Amid the rocks and caves did He find shelter,
    Drink where the runnels run?
Did the bee lead Him to her hoard of honey
    When the long fast was done?

What were His meditations there we know not,
   And words will not reveal
To lower souls what in its highest moments
   The holiest soul may feel.

He went into the wilderness, thus making
   A solemn pause between
The life divine which He must now accomplish,
   And that where He had been.

The Son of Mary, subject unto Joseph,
   And subject unto her;
At Joseph's craft among the workmen working,
   A village carpenter.

With bearing wood His hands have done for ever,
   Until the cross they bear;
With driving nails, until the nails are driven
   His tender hands that tear.

The Well-Beloved, the Father had declared Him,
   His mission had begun,
And now He must arise and bring His brethren
   To Him, who called Him Son.

CHRIST PERFORMING MIRACLES.

Full of mercy, full of love,
Look upon us from above,
Thou who taught the blind man's night
To entertain a double light,
Thine and the day's (and that Thine too);
The lame away his crutches threw;
The parchèd crust of leprosy,
Returned unto its infancy,
The dumb amazèd was, to hear
His unchained tongue to strike his ear,
Thy powerful mercy did e'en chase
The devil from his usurpèd place,
Where Thou Thyself shouldst dwell, not he,
Oh let Thy love our pattern be!
Let Thy mercy teach one brother
To forgive and love another,
They, copying Thy mercy here,
Thy goodness may hereafter rear
Our souls unto Thy glory—when
Our dust shall cease to be with men.

SAINT JOHN THE BAPTIST BEHEADED.

Soft the summer sun is sinking through the saffron sky to
rest:
Soft the veil of sultry vapour trembles on the desert's breast;
Golden, crimson, purple, opal lights and shadows, warp and
woof,
Wrap the sands in change, and flush Machærus' battlemented
roof,
Saying, " 'Tis my last," a captive rose from the cold dungeon
floor,
Clank'd the fetters with his rising, lean'd the grated lattice
o'er,—
Gaunt albeit in manhood's prime, as he through bitter toils
had pass'd,
"One look more on earthly sunsets; my heart tells me, 'tis
the last."

In his eye the fading sunlight linger'd on as loth to go,
Light to light akin and kindling, brotherlike; and to and fro,
As the winds crept o'er the desert from the hills of Abarim,
From his brow his unshorn tresses flutter'd in the twilight dim.
Now and then a passing glory from the castle's banquet hall,
Where a thousand lamps bade thousand guests to royal festival,
Smote the topmost turrets' ridges with a gleam of fitful light,
As the woven purple hangings, sail-like, caught the gales of
night:
Now and then a gush of laughter; now and then a snatch of
song,
Seem'd to mock the prisoner's vigil, and to do his silence
wrong.
Never a word spake he; but, gazing on the hills and skies and
stars,
Free in thought, as Arab ranger, maugre manacles and bars,
Lived again his life, its daybreak with no childish pastimes
boon,
Morning, midday, and now evening, ere it well was afternoon.

Meet his early homestead: westward of that sea where plies
no skiff,
On the bare bleak upland, nestling only to the rugged cliff,
Far from all the noise of cities, far from all their idle mirth,
Where God's voice was heard in whispers, and the heavens
were near to earth,
There he grew, as grows the lonely pine upon the foreland's
crest,
Fronting tempests, northward, southward, sweep they east, or
sweep they west,

Wrapping round the rocks her roots like iron bands in breadth and length,
Here and there a moss or lichen shedding tenderness on strength.
Thus he grew; the child of age, no brother clasp'd in equal arms,
No sweet sister throwing o'er him the pure magic of her charms;
Heir of all his father's ripe experience both of things and men,
Ripen'd by the mellow suns that shine on threescore years and ten;
Heir of all his saintly mother's burning concentrated love.
Pent for decades and now loosen'd by a mandate from above.
For the rest, no human friendship shared his fellowship with God,
Lonely like the lonely Enoch was the path his spirit trod:
Meet for him whose fearless banner was ere long aloft unfurl'd,
God's ambassador, Christ's herald, in a lapsed and guilty world.

Gliding years passed on; and childhood grew to youth, and youth to prime:
Bodings fill'd the land, and rulers call'd the age a troublous time.
Let it be—all time is troublous; and there is no crystal sea
Betwixt Eden and the trumpet ushering in the great To Be.
Nathless storms were rife, and rumours each the other chased from Rome,
Though their echo knock'd but feebly at the porch of that far home;
And they scarcely stirr'd the pulses in the old man's languid heart,
As he pled the prayer of Simeon, "Let me now in peace depart;"
Scarcely jarr'd the heavenly foretastes of the rapt Elizabeth,
Oft as was her wont repeating, "Welcome life, thrice welcome death."

Droop'd they both with drooping autumn, with the dying year they died,
And in one deep stony chamber slumber sweetly side by side;
But before they slept confided to the Baptist's ear a story,
Richer heir-loom, loftier honour than the wide world's wealth and glory:—
From his sire he heard the marvel of his own predestined birth,
From his mother's lips a mystery which transcends all things of earth.

Now the lonely home was lonelier, now the silence more unmarr'd,
Now his rough-spun dress was rougher, and his hardy fare more hard.

Yet he moved not. God who guided Israel o'er the trackless
waste,
When his hour was come, would call him; and with God there
is no haste.
Meanwhile of all sacred stories, which his bosom fired and
fill'd,
One, the Tishbite, more intensely through and through his
bosom thrill'd.
O that sacrifice on Carmel;—O that fire that fell from
heaven;
O that nation's shout "Jehovah;"—O that bloody stormy
even :—
O that solitary cavern;—O that strong and dreadful wind ;
Rocking earthquake, flames of vengeance ; O that still small
Voice behind :
Those long years of patient witness, crown'd by victory at
last :
Israel's chariot, Israel's horsemen! like a dream the vision
pass'd.
"Would to God the prophet's mantle might but fall upon
my soul !
Would to God a seraph touch me with Esaias' living coal !"

As he pray'd, his soul was troubled with a sudden storm of
thought,
And again was hush'd in silence with profounder feeling
fraught :
And the Spirit's accents,—whether on his mortal ear they fell,
Or without such audience trembled on his spirit, none might
tell,
But they came to him. The altar had been built and piled
and laid :
God himself alone must kindle that which He alone had made.

Through the crowded streets of Salem, see, they whisper
man to man,
Like a flash of summer lightning through the heavens, the
tidings ran :
"In the wilderness by Jordan unto us a Voice is sent,
God is on His way. His herald cries before He comes, Repent."

On the mark of busy traffic, on the merchant's growing
hoard,
On the bridegroom's perfumed chamber, on the banquet's
festive board,
On the halls where pleasure squander'd all the heaps of
avarice,
On the dreams of blind devotion, on the loathsome haunts of
vice,
Like a thunder-roll the tidings fell, and lo ! the sudden gloom
Then and there gave fearful presage of the coming day of
doom.

But the workman left his workshop, and the merchant left
    his wares,
And the miser left his coffers, and the Pharisee his prayers:

From Jerusalem to Jordan, see they pour a motley group,
Young men, maidens, old men, children, priests and people,
    troop on troop:
Neighbour thought not now of neighbour, parent scarcely
    thought of child:
There were few who spoke or answer'd, there were none who
    jeer'd or smiled:
No one wept: tyrannic conscience seal'd their eyes and ears
    and lips,
And Eternity was shadowing Time with terrible eclipse.

There it wound that ancient river: there he stood, that
    lonely man.
Is it yet too late? to rearmost some shrank back, some forward
    ran:
Brave men quail'd, and timid women bolder seem'd beneath
    his eye:
Age grew flush'd, and youth grew paler, and the voice was
    heard to cry,
"God is on His way. The Judge already stands before the
    gate.
Make the lofty low before Him, rugged smooth, and crooked
    straight."

As the multitudes in thousands round him throng'd, a
    timorous flock,
Fell his words like hail in harvest, like the hammer on the
    rock,
Breaking stony hearts to shivers, cloaking, sparing, softening
    nought,
But with lightning flash revealing midnight mysteries of
    thought.
God was Master, man was servant; right was right, and wrong
    was wrong:
Sinners might dream on a little, but the respite was not long.
Good or evil fruit-trees—whether of the twain? no test but
    fruit:
Cut it down; the fire is kindled, and the axe lies at the root.
Wherefore call themselves the children of the God-like
    Abraham?
THINGS THAT ARE alone are precious unto the supreme I AM.
Generation bred of vipers, wherefore are they pale and dumb?
Will they flee? oh, who hath warn'd them of the dreadful
    wrath to come?
Are the dry bones stirring, breathing? God can raise up
    men from stones.

See the Lamb, the dying Victim! only life for life atones ;
And the deep red current, flowing from the firstlings Abel
   vow'd,
Cries from age to age for mercy, louder yet, and yet more loud,
Till the sacrifice be offer'd for the world's stupendous guilt,
And the Lamb of God is smitten on the altar God has built.
Is the hard heart bruised and contrite? Do they weep and
   vow and pray?
It is well; let Jordan's waters wash their loathèd stains away.
But the coming One, whose coming now was every moment
   nigher,
He, the Son of God, baptizes with the Holy Ghost and fire :
In His hand the fan that winnows ; at His feet the harvest
   floor ;
Chaff the food for quenchless burnings; garner'd wheat for
   evermore.

So it was from dawn to sunset, so it was from day to day,
Thousands coming, thousands going till the summer wore
   away :
Ever seem'd the voice more solemn, and the message more
   sublime :
Jordan's lonesome fords were crowded like God's hill at Pas-
   chal time.
When one eve,—the roseate West was watching for the tardy
   sun,—
Mingling with that throng of sinners came the Only Sinless
   One ;
And the Master knelt a suppliant, and abash'd the servant
   stood,
While the holy Christ demanded baptism in that cleansing
   flood.
It is done : Messiah rises from the parted waves ; and lo,
The blue heavens are rent asunder, and a Dove, more white
   than snow,
From the gates of light descending like a crown of glory glow'd,
Moving towards Him, hovering o'er Him, brooding on His
   head, abode :
And a Voice more deep than thunder from the everlasting
   Throne,
"Thou, my Son, my well Beloved, Thou art my delight alone."

This the Baptist heard. And straightway Love Divine his soul
   possess'd.
Henceforth all his yearning spirit found its centre, knew its
   rest.
Solitudes no more were lonely, wildernesses were not wild :
He had seen the Word-Incarnate, seen the Father's Holy Child.
And the pure ideal imaged in his heart of hearts was such
That no earthly joys could dim it, and no human sorrows touch.

Let the vex'd waves surge around him! Welcome weariness
    and strife;
Christ was now his peace, his passion—the one passion of his
    life.
He must decrease, Christ must increase, and His kingdom
    know no end,
He had heard the Bridegroom's accents, he was call'd the
    Bridegroom's friend.
Be it that his days were number'd; this was joy enough for
    him;
And his cup of life was mantling to the overflowing brim.
Let his lamp grow pale and paler; only let the Sun be bright,
And the day-star hide its radiance in that perfect Light of
    Light.

So his breast grew calm and calmer, less of self and selfish
    leaven;
So the fire burn'd pure and purer, less of earth and more of
    heaven;
And a loftier hope sustain'd him, as his destined path he trod,
Preaching a world-wide salvation, heralding the Lamb of God!
And the voice rang in the palace, as in hovel and in tent,
"Lo the coming One is come: His kingdom is at hand—repent."

Herod heard him, and Herodias, seated on their ivory throne.
Something in them craved an audience, and he spake to them
    alone;
Spake of sin and death and judgment, things done wrong and
    undone things.
What to him a royal sinner? He had seen the King of kings!
Herod trembled: deeds of rapine cluster'd round his bygone
    path,
Spectres of departed passions, harbingers of coming wrath.
Bid them all avaunt for ever! Blot them from his feverish
    view!
Still forgotten crimes are rising, and his tortured soul pursue.
He will doff his purple robes, in sackcloth and in ashes lie.
What is time? A day dream Oh, that burning word,
    eternity!
Not enough? Why looks the Baptist with that fix'd and
    solemn gaze?
Gold and silver, pearls and rubies, on the temple gate shall
    blaze.
Not enough? Why looks the Baptist piercing through his
    soul and life?
Ha! the queen, his royal consort! nay, his brother Philip's
    wife.
Herod shrank, but smiled Herodias, though the gathering
    vengeance drain'd
Lip of blood, and cheek of blushes. Further answer she
    disdain'd,

But arose, drew forth the monarch, said their royal tryst was
    o'er ;
And that night in chains the Baptist pressed Machærus'
    dungeon floor.

Thrice since then had spring and summer carpeted the earth
    with flowers :
But those dreary walls unchanging fenced his slow and
    changeless hours,
Save there grew 'twixt blocks of granite from some chance-
    sown seed, a fern ;
And the captive watched it ever with the daylight's first
    return,
Drinking in the earliest sunbeam, beaded with its dewy tears,
All its tender leaflets laden and emboss'd for future years.
And it spake to him. It chanced there visited his lonely
    cell,
Chuza, seneschal of Herod ; and a word of power that fell
From the Baptist's lips found lodgment in the deep repose
    of thought
Hidden in a kindred nature, truthful, generous, nobly wrought.
So it was, an unknown friendship unsuspected entrance gains
For a love that loved their master better, dearer for his chains :
Whence he knew ONE name was wafted now on every passing
    breath,
Filling Judea's hills and valleys with the fame of Nazareth.
Joy for thee ! no weak reed shaken by the fickle, fitful wind :
No soft courtier clothed in raiment woven in the looms of
    Ind :
O true prophet, more than prophet ! voice of God ! Messiah's
    friend !
Burning, shining, let thy beacon blaze unwavering to the end !

* * * * * * * *

Musing thus his past, the captive on his watch nor slept
    nor stirr'd,
And the hours slid by unheeded, and the cock crew twice
    unheard ;
And the dewy stars more faintly glimmer'd in the doubtful
    gloom,
And the bursts of mirth were fewer from the royal banquet
    room.

Thither Galilee had summon'd all her loveliness and state,
And her loveliest there seem'd lovelier, and her greatness
    there more great :
Flow'd the purple wine like water : Eden's perfumes fill'd the
    hall ;
And the lamps through roseate colours shed a soften'd light
    on all.
Mirth and music hand in hand were floating through the fairy
    scene ;

All were praising Herod's glory, all were lauding Herod's queen;
When at given sign was silence, and the guests reclined around,
And a lonely harper, waking from the chords a dreamlike sound,
Breathed delight and soft enchantment over ear and heart and soul :
None could choose but list, and listening, none their tenderest thoughts control :
When the young, the fair Salomè, from her chamber gently slid,
Nor loose veil, nor golden tresses half her mantling blushes hid :
Young Salomè, sixteen summers scarcely on her bloom had smiled;
Art was none, but artless beauty; Nature's simplest, fondest child.
At the banquet's edge she linger'd, to her mother's side she press'd,
And assay'd to dance, and falter'd trembling — but again caress'd,
As those wild notes with a stronger witchery on her spirit fell,
Stole into the midst, and startled, timid as a young gazelle,
Trod the air with printless footsteps, as the breezes tread the sea,
Moved to every tone responsive, like embodied melody :
Till embolden'd, as she floated like a cloud of light along,
Mingled with melodious music gentler cadences of song,
And when every ear was ravish'd, every heart subdued with love,
Dropp'd at length, as drops the skylark from its azure home above,
Swiftly with an angel's swiftness, with a mortal's sweetness sweet,
Glowing, trembling, trusting, loving — dropp'd at length at Herod's feet.

Heaven be witness, Herod grants her the petition she prefers :
Half his kingdom were mean dowry for a loveliness like hers.

To Herodias young Salomè fondly turns, with grateful smiles :
Gold of Ophir, pearls of ocean, nard and spice of happier isles,—
What of choice and costly treasures, choicest, costliest, shall she claim ?
Then a glare of fiendish triumph in that cruel cold eye came;
And the queen's heart heaved with vengeance; and she gasp'd with quicken'd breath,
Brief words of envenom'd malice, warrant of the prophet's death.

Why that sudden ashy pallor ? why that passionate caress ?
Bends the sapling in the tempest : weakness yields to wickedness.
　•　　•　　•　　•　　•　　•　　•

Musing till his past, the captive on his watch nor slept nor stirr'd,
And the dawn drew on unheeded, and the cock crew thrice unheard.
Of the sentinels of morning, shining over Abarim,
Only one was left, the Day-star ; and its lamp was growing dim.
Hark! the bolt in drawn, how slowly : see! the dungeon door flung wide :
Weapons gleam along the passage : armèd men are by his side.
In their looks he read his sentence, and he knew his hour was come,
And his proud neck meekly offer'd to the stroke of martyrdom :
And, as flash'd the headman's broadsword, rose the sun on Pisgah's height ;
And the morning star was hidden in the flood of golden light.

THE LEPER.

"Room for the leper! room!" And as he came,
The cry passed on—"Room for the leper! room!"
Sunrise was slanting on the city gates
Rosy and beautiful, and from the hills
The early-risen poor were coming in,
Duly and cheerfully, to their toil, and up
Rose the sharp hammer's clink, and the far hum
Of moving wheels and multitudes astir,
And all that in a city murmur swells,
Unheard but by the watcher's weary ear,
Aching with night's dull silence, or the sick
Hailing the welcome light, and sounds that chase
The death-like images of the dark away.
"Room for the leper!" And aside they stood,
Matron, and child, and pitiless manhood—all
Who met him on his way—and let him pass.
And onward through the open gate he came
A leper, with the ashes on his brow,
Sackcloth about his loins, and on his lip
A covering, stepping painfully and slow,
And with a difficult utterance, like one
Whose heart is with an iron nerve put down,
Crying, "Unclean! Unclean!"

'Twas now the depth
Of the Judæan summer, and the leaves
Whose shadow lay so still upon the path,
Had budded on the clear and flashing eye
Of Judah's loftiest noble. He was young,
And eminently beautiful, and life
Mantled in eloquent fulness on his lip,
And sparkled in his glance; and in his mien
There was a gracious pride that every eye
Followed with benisons—and this was he!
With the soft air of summer there had come
A torpor on his frame, which not the speed
Of his best barb, nor music, nor the blast
Of the bold huntsman's horn, nor aught that stirs
The spirit to its bent, might drive away.
The blood beat not as wont within his veins;
Dimness crept o'er his eye; a drowsy sloth
Fettered his limbs like palsy, and his port,
With all his loftiness, seemed struck with eld.
Even his voice was changed—a languid moan
Taking the place of the clear, silver key;
And brain and sense grew faint, as if the light,
And very air, were steeped in sluggishness,
He strove with it awhile, as manhood will,
Ever too proud for weakness, till the rein
Slackened within his grasp, and in its poise
The arrowy jereed like an aspen shook.
Day after day he lay as if in sleep;
His skin grew dry and bloodless, and white scales
Circled with livid purple, covered him.
And then his nails grew black, and fell away
From the dull flesh about them, and the hues
Deepened beneath the hard unmoistened scales,
And from their edges grew the rank white hair,
—And Helon was a leper!

Day was breaking
When at the altar of the temple stood
The holy priest of God. The incense lamp
Burned with a struggling light, and a low chant
Swelled through the hollow arches of the roof
Like an articulate wail, and there alone,
Wasted to ghastly thinness, Helon knelt.
The echoes of the melancholy strain
Died in the distant aisles, and he rose up,
Struggling with weakness, and bowed down his head
Unto the sprinkled ashes, and put off
His costly raiment for the leper's garb,
And with the sackcloth round him, and his lip
Hid in a loathsome covering, stood still,
Waiting to hear his doom:—

Depart! depart! O child
Of Israel, from the temple of thy God,
For He has smote thee with his chastening rod,
   And to the desert wild,
From all thou lovest, away thy feet must flee,
That from thy plague His people may be free.

   Depart, and come not near
The busy mart, the crowded city, more;
Nor set thy foot a human threshold o'er.
   And stay thou not to hear
Voices that call thee in the way; and fly
From all who in the wilderness pass by.

   Wet not thy burning lip
In streams that to a human dwelling glide:
Nor rest thee where the covert fountains bide;
   Nor kneel thee down to dip
The water where the pilgrim bends to drink,
By desert well, or river's grassy brink.

   And pass not thou between
The weary traveller and the cooling breeze,
And lie not down to sleep beneath the trees
   Where human tracks are seen;
Nor milk the goat that browseth on the plain,
Nor pluck the standing corn, or yellow grain.

   And now depart and when
Thy heart is heavy, and thine eyes are dim,
Lift up thy prayer beseechingly to Him
   Who, from the tribes of men,
Selected thee to feel his chastening rod.
Depart, oh leper! and forget not God!

   And he went forth—alone; not one, of all
The many whom he loved, nor she whose name
Was woven in the fibres of the heart
Breaking within him now, to come and speak
Comfort unto him. Yea, he went his way,
Sick, and heart-broken, and alone, to die;
For God hath cursed the leper!

                                 It was noon,
And Helon knelt beside a stagnant pool
In the lone wilderness, and bathed his brow,
Hot with the burning leprosy, and touched
The loathsome water to his parchèd lips,
Praying that he might be so blessed—to die!
Footsteps approached, and with no strength to flee,
He drew the covering closer on his lip,
Crying, "Unclean! Unclean!" and, in the folds

Of the coarse sackcloth, shrouding up his face,
He fell upon the earth till they should pass.
Nearer the stranger came, and bending o'er
The leper's prostrate form, pronounced his name,
—"Helon!"—the voice was like the master-tone
Of a rich instrument—most strangely sweet;
And the dull pulses of disease awoke,
And for a moment beat beneath the hot
And leprous scales with a restoring thrill.
"Helon, arise!" and he forget his curse,
And rose and stood before Him.

        Love and awe
Mingled in the regard of Helon's eye
As he beheld the stranger. He was not
In costly raiment clad, nor on His brow
The symbol of a princely lineage wore;
No followers at His back, nor in His hand
Buckler, or sword, or spear;—yet in His mien
Command sat throned serene, and, if He smiled,
A kindly condescension graced His lips,
The lion would have crouched to in his lair;
His garb was simple, and His sandals worn;
His statue modelled with a perfect grace;
His countenance, the impress of a God,
Touched with the open innocence of a child;
His eye was blue and calm, as is the sky
In the serenest noon; His hair unshorn,
Fell on His shoulders; and His curling beard
The fulness of perfected manhood bore.
He looked on Helon earnestly awhile,
As if His heart was moved, and stooping down.
He took a little water in His hand,
And laid it on his brow, and said, "Be clean!"
And lo! the scales fell from him, and his blood
Coursed with delicious coolness through his veins,
And his dry palms grew moist, and on his brow
The dewy softness of an infant stole.
His leprosy was cleansed, and he fell down
Prostrate at Jesus' feet, and worshipped Him.

THE WIDOW OF NAIN.

She saw him—Death's untimely prey,
 Struck with the blight of slow decline:
She watched his vigour waste away,
 His ardent spirit droop and pine.

The rose upon his cheek, she knew,
Bloomed not with health's transparent hue;
It was a softer, fainter glow—
  A tint of fading loveliness,
Which told, a canker lurked below:
So gleams o'er fields of wintry snow
  The pale moon cold and comfortless.
And oft she marked within his eye
A wild unwonted brilliancy—
The lovely but delusive ray
Of nature sinking to decay;
And oft she caught his stifled moan—
It breathed a deep and hollow tone,
Which told of death, e'er life was gone.
At times, when fever's burning flush
Heightened consumption's hectic blush,
Fond hope—the latest still to leave,
The first to flatter and deceive—
Once more would brighten—but to fly
  When that false flush forsook his cheek,
  And spoke the pang he would not speak,
And froze her fears to certainty.
Nor deem it strange, that hope had power
To soothe her soul in such an hour;
Where time has rent the lordly tower,
  And moss entwines the arches gray,
Springs many a light and lovely flower
  That lends a lustre to decay.
Thus, while existence wanes away,
Consumption's fevered cheek will bloom,
  And beauty's brightest beams will play,
In mournful glory o'er the tomb.
  *   *   *   *   *

Whate'er his inward pangs might be,
  He told not—mute, and meekly still
  He bowed him to Jehovah's will,
Nor murmured at the stern decree;
For gently falls the chastening rod
On him whose hope is in his God:
For her, too, who beside his bed
  Still watched with fond maternal care,
  For her he breathed the pious prayer—
The tear of love and pity shed,
Oft would he bid her try to rest,
  And turn his pallid face away,
  Lest some unguarded look betray
The pangs nor sigh nor sound expressed.
When torture racked his breast, 'twas known
By sudden shivering starts alone;
Yet would *her* searching glance espy
The look of stifled agony—

For what can 'scape a mother's eye ?
She deemed in health she loved him more
Than ever mother loved before ;
But oh ! when thus in cold decay,
So placid, so resigned he lay,
And she beheld him waste away,
And marked that gentle tenderness
Which watched and wept for *her* distress :
Then did her transient firmness melt
To tears of love, more deeply felt :
And dearer still he grew—and dearer—
E'en as the day of death drew nearer.

THE WIDOW OF NAIN.

Wake not, O mother, sounds of lamentation !
  Weep not, O widow, weep not hopelessly !
Strong is His arm, the Bringer of Salvation,
  Strong is the Word of God to succour thee !

Bear forth the cold corpse, slowly bear him :
  Hide his pale features with the sable pall :
Chide not the sad one wildly weeping near him :
  Widow'd and childless, she had lost her all !

Why pause the mourners ? Who forbids our weeping ?
  Who the dark pomp of sorrow has delay'd ?
"Set down the bier—he is not dead but sleeping :
  Young man, arise !"—He spake, and was obey'd !

Change then, O sad one ! grief to exultation ;
  Worship and fall before Messiah's knee ;
Strong was His arm, the Bringer of Salvation :
  Strong was the Word of God to succour thee !

MARY MAGDALENE.

Low at the Saviour's feet a guilty sinner bends ;
  Up to His loving face a tearful glance she sends :
" Can one Himself so pure, of lineage so high,
  The loathsome sight endure of one so vile as I ? "

Around His weary feet her loving arms are cast,
   Whilst tears of sorrow sweet fall o'er them thick and fast;
Her long and flowing hair—the pride of woman's eye,
   Is not esteem'd too fair to cleanse and wipe them dry.

How doth each warm caress her clinging lips impart,
   In language mute express the yearnings of her heart?
That ointment rich and rare her poverty could bring—
   Its odours sweet declare 'tis no mean offering.

The Pharisee and Scribe, exalted in their pride,
   Can gaze in silent scorn, or turn their eyes aside;
Can gather up their robes, and feign a pious fear,
   Lest they should be defil'd e'en by her passing near;

But from " the Sinner's Friend "—her gracious loving Lord—
   No scornful looks descend, no proud, no angry word:
" Can He a prophet be," their wond'ring looks would say—
   " And suffer such as she within His sight to stay?"

" Yes, sepulchres of sin! who, whited fairly o'er,
   Are dark and foul within, and rotten at the core;
Yes, His keen gaze can pierce each human bosom through,
   And to His searching eyes she's purer far than you!

" She whom the righteous spurn—whom Publicans revile—
   Whom sin's most loathsome marks deface, degrade, defile;
Though on her guilty soul be many a deep, foul stain,
   Her faith in Jesus' blood shall wash it pure again!

" But you—your lengthy pray'rs, hypocrisy and pride,
   Long robes and public alms, your God will not abide:
You have your poor reward in man's approving look,
   But His indignant wrath such insult cannot brook."

" Proud host, to thy high guest no water gavest thou;
   Thou gavest Him no kiss on pallid cheek or brow:
Not even olive oil didst thou vouchsafe to shed,
   In sweetly-soothing streams, upon that holy head.

" But she, with gushing tears, hath wash'd His wayworn feet;
   And hath not ceas'd to press fond kisses soft and sweet:
With those fair-flowing locks which grace her downcast head,
   Those feet were fondly dried—with rarest ointment spread."

" Ye Pharisaic tribe, who boast yourselves so clear
   From sin's polluting stains, look to your souls, and fear!
Ye feel no need of mercy, but claim a place above;
   And thus for Christ your Saviour, how little is your love!

" But ye who, bow'd with sin, have counted Jesus dear,
   Ye in whose hearts the streams of love run deep and clear,—
Look, penitents, to Heaven! the Saviour loveth such—
   " To you much is forgiven, for you have lovèd much!"

THE MEMORIAL OF MARY.

Thou hast thy record in the monarch's hall,
  And on the waters of the far mid sea;
And where the mighty mountain-shadows fall,
  The Alpine hamlet keeps a thought of thee;
Where'er, beneath some Oriental tree,
The Christian traveller rests—where'er the child
  Looks upward from the English mother's knee,
With earnest eye in wondering reverence mild,
There art thou known—where'er the Book of Light
Bears hope and healing, there, beyond all blight,
  Is borne thy memory, and all praise above :
Oh! say what deed so lifted thy sweet name,
Mary! to that pure silent place of fame?
  One lowly offering of exceeding love.

THE NIGHT IN GALILEE.

Tossed by the ruthless sea,
  Driven by the faithless storm,
A little bark right gallantly
  Uprears its little form.
But, in vain it breasts the wave,
  With its puny wings outspread;
No human aid can save
  That bark from a wat'ry bed.

A sickness as of death,
  Seizes the little crew,—
And each man holds his breath,
  For their moments can be but few.
But, amid the thick'ning gloom,
  A spectre seems to rise,
As from the hideous tomb,
  That yawns before their eyes.

And clearer, and more clear,
  That awful vision grows,—
And the wild, shrill cry of fear,
  With the voice of the tempest rose.
But words of love and peace
  Are heard 'mid the storm and dark,—
And Jesus brings release
  To the little sinking bark.

So, oft on the sea of life,
  When our little bark is tossed,
And amid foul passions' strife,
  Our every hope seems lost,
Jesus is walking near
  To still each rising wave,—
Our drooping hearts to cheer,—
  Our drowning souls to save.

CHRIST STILLING THE TEMPEST.

The storm was loud, the ship was tossed
  On dark Gennesareth;
Their faith the twelve Apostles lost,
  When face to face with death.

But safe they were in their alarm
  Upon that raging sea,
No angry wind nor wave could harm
  Those who were dear to Thee.

And ever in the darkest night,
  And in the wildest hour,
Thy love, oh Lord, can bring me light,
  Thy voice put forth its power.

Light which, in shining, will impart
  A holy joy and peace,
Power which can still the restless heart,
  And bid the tempest cease.

Why should this fluttering heart have fear
  In darkness or in death,
While Thou my Saviour still art near,
  To help its trembling faith?

Why doubt as if Thou couldst deceive,
  Why droop in hopeless grief,
While I can cry — Lord I believe,
  Oh help my unbelief?

THE RAISING OF THE DAUGHTER OF JAIRUS.

THE same silvery light
That shone upon the lone rock by the sea,
Slept on the ruler's lofty capitals,
As at the door he stood, and welcomed in
Jesus and his disciples. All was still.
The echoing vestibule gave back the slide
Of their loose sandals, and the arrowy beam
Of moonlight, slanting to the marble floor,
Lay like a spell of silence in the rooms,
As Jairus led them on.

With hushing steps
He trod the winding stair; but ere he touched
The latchet, from within a whisper came,
"Trouble the master not; for she is dead!"
And his faint hand fell nerveless at his side,
And his step faltered, and his broken voice
Choked in its utterance; but a gentle hand
Was laid upon his arm, and in his ear
The Saviour's voice sunk thrillingly and low,
"She is not dead, but sleepeth."

They passed in.
The spice-lamps in the alabaster urns
Burned dimly, and the white and fragrant smoke
Curled indolently on the chamber walls;
The silken curtains slumbered in their folds,—
Not even a tassel stirring in the air,—
And, as the Saviour stood beside the bed,
And prayed inaudibly, the ruler heard
The quickening division of His breath
As He grew earnest inwardly. There came
A gradual brightness o'er His calm, sad face;
And drawing nearer to the bed, He moved
The silken curtains silently apart,
And looked upon the maiden.

Like a form
Of matchless sculpture in her sleep she lay,—
The linen vesture folded on her breast,
And over it her white transparent hands,
The blood still rosy in their tapering nails.
A line of pearl ran through her parted lips,
And in her nostrils spiritually thin,
The breathing curve was mockingly like life;

And round beneath the faintly tinted skin
Ran the light branches of the azure veins;
And on her cheek the jet lash overlay,
Matching the arches penciled on her brow.
Her hair had been unbound, and falling loose
Upon her pillow, hid her small round ears
In curls of glossy blackness, and about
Her polished neck, scarce touching it, they hung,
Like airy shadows floating as they slept.
'Twas heavenly beautiful.

    The Saviour raised
Her hand from off her bosom, and spread out
The snowy fingers in His palm, and said,
" Maiden! arise!" and suddenly a flash
Shot o'er her forehead, and along her lips
And through her cheek the rallied colour ran;
And the still outline of her graceful form
Stirred in the linen vesture; and she clasped
The Saviour's hand, and, fixing her dark eyes
Full on His beaming countenance,—AROSE !

THE RAISING OF THE DAUGHTER OF JAIRUS.

THEY have watched her last and quivering breath,
 And the maiden's soul has flown;
They have wrapt her in the robes of death,
 And laid her dark and alone.

But the mother casts a look behind,
 Upon that fallen flower,—
Nay, start not,—'twas the gathering wind :
 Those limbs have lost their power.

And tremble not at that cheek of snow,
 O'er which the faint light plays ;
'Tis only the crimson curtain's glow,
 Which thus deceives thy gaze.

Didst thou not close that expiring eye,
 And feel the soft pulse decay!
And did not thy lips receive the sigh,
 Which bore her soul away?

She lies on her couch, all pale and hushed,
 And heeds not thy gentle tread,

And is still as the spring flower by traveller crushed,
  Which dies on its snowy bed.

The mother has flown from that lonely room,
  And the maid is mute and pale :
Her ivory hand is cold as the tomb,
  And dark is her stiffened nail.

Her mother strays with folded arms,
  And her head is bent in woe ;
She shuts her thoughts to joy or charms !
  Nor tear attempts to flow.

But listen ! what name salutes her ear ?
  It comes to a heart of stone ;
"Jesus," she cries, "has no power here ;
  My daughter's life has flown."

He leads the way to that cold white couch,
  And bends o'er the senseless form ;
Can His be less than a heavy touch ?
  The maiden's hand is warm !

And the fresh blood comes with a roseate hue,
  While Death's dark terrors fly;
Her form is raised, and her step is true,
  And life beams bright in her eye.

THE WOMAN OF CANAAN.

Prayer an answer will obtain,
  Though the Lord awhile delay,
None shall seek His face in vain,
  None be empty sent away.

When the woman came from Tyre,
  And for help to Jesus sought,
Though He granted her desire,
  Yet, at first, He answered not.

Could she guess at His intent,
  When He to His followers said, —
"I to Israel's sheep am sent,
  Dogs must not have the children's bread ?"

She was not of Israel's seed,
  But of Canaan's wretched race ;

Thought herself a dog indeed —
Was not this a hopeless case?

Yet, although from Canaan sprung,
  Though a dog herself she styled,
She had Israel's faith and tongue,
  And was owned by Abram's child.

From His word she draws a plea,
  Though unworthy children's bread,
'Tis enough for one like me,
  If with crumbs I may be fed.

Jesus then His heart revealed,
  "Woman, cans't thou thus believe?
I to thy petition yield
  All that thou cans't wish, receive."

'Tis a pattern set for us,
  How we ought to wait and pray;
None who plead and wrestle thus,
  Will be empty sent away.

THE TRANSFIGURATION.

In days of old on Sinai
  The Lord Almighty came,
In majesty of terror,
  In thunder-cloud and flame:
On Tabor, with the glory
  Of sunniest light for vest,
The excellence of beauty
  In Jesus was expressed.

All light created palèd there,
  And did Him worship meet:
The sun itself adorèd Him,
  And bowed before His feet:
While Moses and Elias,
  Upon the Holy Mount,
The co-eternal glory
  Of Christ our God recount.

O holy, wondrous vision!
  But what, when, this life past,
The beauty of Mount Tabor
  Shall end in heaven at last?
But what, when all the glory
  Of uncreated light
Shall be the promised guerdon
  Of them that win the fight?

10

THE TEN LEPERS.

'NEATH the olives of Samaria, in far-famed Galilee,
Where dark green vines are mirrored in a placid silver sea,
'Mid scenes of tranquil beauty, glowing sun-sets, rosy dawn,
The Master and Disciples to Jerusalem journeyed on.

And behold, as they were entering a hamlet still and fair,
A strange, imploring wailing rang out on the quiet air ;
Voices fraught with anguish, telling of aching heart and brow,
And they moaned forth " Jesus, Master, on us have mercy
    now ! "

Softly raised the gentle Saviour His eyes like midnight star,
And His mournful gaze quick rested on ten lepers, who, afar,
Stood motionless and suppliant, in sackcloth rudely clothed,
Poor pariahs ! by their nearest, their dearest, shunned and
    loathed.

Not unto Him prayed vainly, those sore-afflicted ten,
Ah ! He yearned too fondly over the erring sons of men:
Ever sharing in their sorrows, though He shunned their
    mirthful feasts,
Kindly now He told the lepers, "Show yourselves unto the
    priests."

When, miracle of mercy ! as they turned them to obey,
And towards the holy Temple quickly take their hopeful way,
Lo, the hideous scales fell off them, health's fountains were
    unsealed,
Their skin grew soft as infants — their leprosy was healed.

Oh! man, so oft an ingrate, to thy thankless nature true,
Thyself, see in those lepers who did as thou dost do ;
Nine went their way rejoicing, healed in body — glad in soul—
Nor thought of once returning to thank Him who made them
    whole.

One only, a Samaritan, a stranger to God's word,
Felt his joyous, panting bosom, with gratitude deep stirred,
And without delay he hastened, in the dust at Jesus' feet,
To cast himself in worship, in thanksgiving warm and meet.

Slowly questioned him, then Jesus, with majesty divine,
" Ten were cleansèd from their leprosy—where are the other
    nine ?
Is there none but this one stranger—unlearnèd in God's ways,
His name or mighty power, to give word of thanks or praise ? "

The sunbeams' quivering glories softly touched that God-like head,
The olives blooming round Him, sweet shade and fragrance shed,
Whilst o'er His sacred features, a tender sadness stole,
"Rise, go thy way," He murmured, "thy faith hath made thee whole!"

LAZARUS.

PALE was his brow, his flashing eye
Had fever's restless brilliancy!
The burning flush of hectic bloom,
But whisper'd of the hastening tomb;
The quivering lip all vainly strove
To breathe the wonted tones of love,
Yet trembled in a voiceless prayer
To Him, the Almighty Comforter.

He was the loved of many a heart,
O was he doom'd with all to part?
His bright young brow with hope's fair wreath
  In rich and fragrant loveliness,
Had long been garlanded, nor breath
  Of care awoke to chase
The fairy hues of golden light
That flash'd athwart his pathway bright:
O fair are youth's enchanted dreams!
Its vernal joys, its rainbow gleams!
Its tones of melody that fling
Sweet music as the voice of spring
    Amidst her own bright blossoming!
Yet were they fleeting, as the pride
Of calm yet gorgeous eventide;—
Their beauty as a vision fair,
Was melting in immortal air;
Their melody was hasting by,
A dream alone of memory.
But glories of a brighter shore
That sufferer's musings glided o'er;
His spirit at life's welling stream
    Had quench'd its thirstings deep,
His heart had hail'd a heavenly beam,
    Had joy'd the fruits to reap
Of peace and holiness that bloom'd

Afresh when earthly hope was tomb'd:
And visions of the land of light
Burst on his raptured, dazzled sight,
The crown, the harp, the starry throne,
The glory of the great Three One!
The angel throng, the seraph lays,
The symphony of ceaseless praise,
The music of unearthly lyres,
The rapture of celestial fires!
What though affection's sweetest ties
Might seek to win him from the skies!
Fond eyes of love with tearful rays
Rest on him in deep earnest gaze;
Sad tones from kindred bosoms speak
Of hearts that sorrow nigh did break;
Wild, bursting sobs of anguish tell
Of love unknown, unsearchable;
Yet was his heart his treasure high,
In climes of immortality!

A sister's love! that hallow'd light
Who, who may quench in rayless night?
Have we not shared one childhood's home,
One bower where sorrow might not come?
Have we not round one happy hearth
Our bright hopes mingled, and our mirth?
Have we not the same fond eyes of love
Watch'd o'er our cradle-rest, whilst wove
Bright Fancy many a wreath of hope,
In love's deep shrine to treasure up?
Have we not bent in twilight's hour,
Our simple orison to pour,
To Him who o'er our vernal way
Had flung a pure, a heavenly ray?
Have not our young gay dreams of light,
Ere time their loveliness might blight,
Together blent, while each glad hour,
Breeze, sunshine, fragrancy, and shower,
Shed on their joyousness, and bade
Them glow as ne'er in gloom to fade?
O sacred is that spell! a light
Flung o'er life's changeful pilgrimage:
A star amid its care's deep night!
  A balm its sorrow to assuage!

Such love around the sufferer clung:
Fond hearts, by withering anguish wrung,
Bent o'er his weary couch, as fain
To banish agony: yet vain
Each sister's sorrowing tenderness,
Each throb of anguish and distress!

But must they part? The love of years,
The mingled joys, and hopes, and fears,
Long blended in each kindred heart,—
O must they prove the severing dart?
Deep love! above the radiant sky
Lift up thy mourning, tearful eye!
Thou hast no dwelling-place below,
Where sin and sorrow, care and woe,
May blight not with their mildew breath
The brightest of thy treasured wreath!
'Tis past! e'en hope must vanish now!
Upon the bright and youthful brow,
Where raven locks in clustering pride,
Its marble paleness seek to hide,
Is set the signet stamp of death;
The weary pulse, the quivering breath,
The gushing purple flood of life,
The sigh, the tear, the mortal strife,
Have ceased,—and on the drooping eye
The grave's dark shadow mournfully,
Hath fallen in the violet gloom
That speaks but of the quiet tomb.
Young life hath pass'd, away! away!
The loved, the cherish'd,—he is clay!

* * *

Eve on the steeps of Judah's hills
Her golden light was streaming;
The melody of sounding rills
  Amid the olives gleaming,
But lent to stillness deeper power,
And flung a charm o'er sunset's hour.
Within their lonely, silent home,
The mourners wept in hopeless gloom;
The voice that to their spirits brought
A thrill of happiness e'er sought;
The eye, whose radiant glance of light
Might chase the clouds of sorrow's night;
The heart that shared their every woe,
All, all, alas! in dust lay low.
Around them stood a sorrowing band,
Who strove the balm to pour,
That friendship's eye, and heart, and hand,
  On stricken ones would shower;
Still, still they wept: O to their grief
What earthly power might bring relief?
E'en sympathy's unutter'd spell
But proved the lost one loved too well?
Lo! tidings of a guest revered,
By more than human ties endear'd,
Is to the house of mourning borne,

And o'er the sisters' hearts forlorn.
Doth rush the whelming thought — had He
The stranger, at their loved one's side
Stood in the hour of agony,
  He had not in his spring-morn died!
Too late! the mortal pang was o'er,
Nor aught might wake the sleeper more!
Yet hastens Martha, swift to greet
Her Lord and Master;—at His feet
She fell, and breathed her woe's deep tide,
"Hadst Thou been here, he had not died!"
O was it but a joyous dream
That flung a bright yet trembling gleam
O'er her dark spirit's midnight gloom,
That bade it rise above the tomb?

One moment and a weeping band
Around the pitying Saviour stand;
In vain the mourners strive to stem
Their hopeless grief,—doth He condemn?
Or bid the sorrowing cease to shed
The tear of anguish o'er the dead?
No! in His spirit's depths He groans.
While weeping Mary's piercing moans
Thrill'd to His bosom's inmost shrine,
And He, the Incarnate God Divine,
The Lord of Life, His throne who left
For earth's sad sojourn,—lo, He wept!

O He had known the cherish'd ties
That link fond human sympathies!
And oft with him who lowly laid
Within the dark grave's rayless shade,
Had blent in converse sacred,—sweet,
In communing for bright worlds meet.
"He loved him!" hallow'd is the spell
Affection o'er the soul doth fling,
Since He, the God Invisible,
  Disdain'd not its deep communing!
They led Him to the rock-hewn bed
Where slept in dreamless rest the dead:
Athwart its stillness deep were thrown
The shadows of a gloom more lone.
Why doth He bid the circling group
The stone from that dark cell lift up?
Hath not decay its victim found?
Hath not the worm its pale form wound?
What recks it? 'Tis the word of Him
Who spake the world from chaos dim!
The cave is oped, and to the skies
The Saviour lifts His pleading eyes.

Then with a voice of heavenly might
He bids the dead awake to light!
And he the loved, the wept, the mourn'd,
To life and beauty hath return'd!
Hath 'scaped from death's relentless hand,
And bendeth with the adoring band!

THE RAISING OF LAZARUS.

'Tis still thine hour, O Death!
Thine, Lord of Hades, is the kingdom still;
Yet twice thy sword unstained hath sought its sheath,
Though twice upraised to kill;
And once again the tomb
Shall yield its captured prey;
A mightier arm shall pierce the pathless gloom,
And rend the prize away:
Nor comes thy Conqueror armed with spear or sword —
He hath no arms but Prayer — no weapon but His Word.

'Tis now the fourth sad morn
Since Lazarus, the pious and the just,
To his last home by sorrowing kinsmen borne
Hath parted, dust to dust.
The grave-worm revels now
Upon his mouldering clay —
And He, before whose car the mountains bow —
The rivers roll away
In conscious awe — He only can revive
Corruption's withering prey, and call the dead to live!

Yet still the sisters keep
Their sad and silent vigil at the grave,
Watching for Jesus — "Comes He not to weep?
He did not come to save!"
But now *one* straining eye
Th' advancing Form hath traced:—
And soon, in wild, resistless agony
Have Martha's arms embraced
The Saviour's feet — "O Lord! hadst thou been nigh —
But speak the word e'en now, it shall be heard on high!"

● They led Him to the cave —
The rocky bed, where now in darkness slept
Their brother, and His friend — then at the grave
They paused — for "JESUS WEPT."

O love, sublime and deep!
O Hand and Heart divine!
He comes to rescue, though He deigns to weep —
The captive is not thine
O Death! thy bands are burst asunder now —
There stands beside the grave a Mightier far than thou.

"Come forth," He cries, "thou dead!"
O God! what means that strange and sudden sound,
That murmurs from the tomb—that ghastly head,
With funeral fillets bound?
It is a LIVING FORM —
The loved, the lost, the won,
Won from the grave, corruption, and the worm —
"And is not this the Son
Of God?" they whispered — while the sisters poured
Their gratitude in tears; for they had known the Lord.

CHRIST BLESSING LITTLE CHILDREN.

"The Master has come over Jordan,"
   Said Hannah, the mother, one day;
"He is healing the people who throng Him,
   With a touch of His finger, they say.

And now I shall carry the children,
   Little Rachel and Samuel and John,
I shall carry the baby Esther,
   For the Lord to look upon."

The father looked at her kindly,
   But he shook his head and smiled;
"Now who but a doting mother
   Would think of a thing so wild?

If the children were tortured by demons,
   Or dying of fever — 'twere well —
Or had they the taint of the leper,
   Like many in Israel."

"Nay, do not hinder me, Nathan,
   I feel such a burden of care, —
If I carry it to the Master,
   Perhaps I shall leave it there.

If He lay His hand on the children,
  My heart will be lighter, I know,
For a blessing for ever and ever
  Will follow them as they go."

So over the hills of Judah,
  Along by the vine-rows green,
With Esther asleep on her bosom,
  And Rachel her brothers between;

'Mong the people who hung on His teaching,
  Or waited His touch and His word,
Through the row of proud Pharisees listening,
  She pressed to the feet of the Lord.

"Now why shouldst thou hinder the Master,"
  Said Peter, "with children like these?
"Seest not how from morning till evening
  He teacheth, and healeth disease?"

Then Christ said, "Forbid not the children,
  Permit them to come unto Me!"
And He took in His arms little Esther,
  And Rachel He sat on His knee;

And the heavy heart of the mother
  Was lifted all earth-care above,
As He laid His hands on the brothers,
  And blest them with tenderest love;

As He said of the babes in His bosom,
  "Of such are the kingdom of heaven"—
And strength for all duty and trial,
  That hour to her spirit was given.

CHRIST BLESSING LITTLE CHILDREN.

It was a lonely village, girt with hills
Beyond the banks of Jordan, where our Lord
Turned from the city, to forego a while
The toils and tumults of Jerusalem.
Nature had quietly and quaintly wrought
In that wild haunt. The gray, primeval rocks
Made solemn contrast to the tender green
That mantled timidly around their base,
And to the slightly rooted shrubs, that sprang
From creft and crevice.

There, a multitude
Followed His footsteps, eager to lay down
The burdens of their mortal misery,
And He, with touch divine, had healed them all.
But then, another differing train drew near,
Whose tread, gazelle-like, told no mournful tale
Of paralytic lore,—and whose bright eyes
Wide open, in their simple wonderment
Revealed unbroken league with health and joy.
Some had been wandering o'er the pasture fields
With the young lambs, and in their tiny hands
Were the blue flax-flower and the lily-buds,
While through the open portals of their hearts,
Sweet odours led sweet thoughts in tireless plays.
Others, from shady lanes and cottage doors,
The dark eyed Jewish mothers, gathering, brought
Unto the feet of Christ.

" Ye may not press
Upon the Master; He is wearied sore;
Hence! Go your way."
So the disciples spake,—
As with impatient gesture they repelled
The approaching groups.
But Jesus, unto whom
The smile of guileless trusting innocence
Was dear, reproved their arrogance, and said,
" Suffer the little ones to come to Me;
Of such as these My Father's kingdom is."
With what high rapture beat the matron heart,
When those fair infants in His sheltering arms
Were folded, and amid their lustrous curls
His hand benignant laid.
Oh, blissful hour!
None save a mother's thrilling love can know
The tide of speechless ecstacy, when those,
Whom she hath brought with pain into the world,
Find refuge with the unforsaking Friend.

Like holiest dews upon the opening flower,
The Saviour's blessing fell.
So sweet its tones
Breathed on the ear, that men of pride and strife,
The venal Scribe and boastful Pharisee,
Started to feel a balm-drop in their souls
Softening the adamant; while humble Faith
Exulted, as, through parting clouds she saw
The children's angels near the Father's throne.

CHRIST'S ENTRY INTO JERUSALEM.

The air is filled with shouts, and trumpets sounding;
A host are at thy gates, Jerusalem,
Now is their van the Mount of Olives rounding;
Observe them, Judah's lion-banners gleam,
Twined with the palm and olive's peaceful stem.
Now swell the nearer sounds of voice and string,
As down the hill-side pours the living stream;
And to the cloudless heaven Hosannas ring—
" The Son of David comes—the Conqueror, the King!"

The cuirassed Roman heard; and grasped his shield,
And rush'd in fiery haste to gate and tower;
The Pontiff from his battlement beheld
The host, and knew the falling of his power,
He saw the cloud on Sion's glory lower,
Still down the marble road the myriads come,
Spreading the way with garment, branch and flower,
And deeper sounds are mingling " woe to Rome!
The day of freedom dawns; rise, Israel, from thy tomb."

Temple of beauty—long that day is done;
Thy wall is dust; thy golden cherubim
In the fierce triumphs of the foe are gone;
The shades of ages on thy altars swim:
Yet still a light is there, though wavering dim;
And has its holy light been watched in vain?
Or lives it not until the finished time,
When He who fixed, shall break His people's chain,
And Sion be the lov'd, the crown'd of God again?

He comes, yet with the burning bolt unarmed;
Pale, pure, prophetic, God of Majesty!
Though thousands, tens of thousands round Him swarm'd,
None durst abide that depth divine of eye;
None durst the waving of His robe draw nigh.
But at His feet was laid the Roman's sword;
There Lazarus knelt to see his King pass by;
There Jairus, with its age's child adored,
" He comes, the King of kings; Hosanna to the Lord!"

CHRIST'S ENTRY INTO JERUSALEM.

Ride on! ride on in majesty!
Hark, all the tribes Hosanna cry!
Thy humble beast pursues his road,
With palms and scartter'd garments strew'd.

Ride on! ride on in majesty!
In lonely pomp ride on to die!
Oh Christ! Thy triumphs now begin
O'er captive death and conquer'd sin.

Ride on! ride on in majesty!
The wingèd squadrons of the sky
Look down, with sad and wondering eyes,
To see the approaching sacrifice!

Ride on! ride on in majesty!
In lowly pomp ride on to die!
Bow Thy meek head to mortal pain,
Then take, O God! Thy power and reign!

CHRIST WEEPING OVER JERUSALEM.

Salem, who in proud disdain,
  My faithful Prophets slew,
And soon, the cup of guilt to drain,
  Wilt slay thy Saviour too.
How had My love thy children blest,
  Their deeds of blood forgot;
And led them to eternal rest?
  But they consented not.

Now shall thy house be desolate,
  Thy glory now shall close,—
Nor leave one trace of ruined state,
  To tell where Salem rose.
Nor shalt thou thy Redeemer see,
  Nor hail thy crown restored;
Till thou shalt say, "How blest is He
  Whom Thou hast sent, O Lord!"

CHRIST COMFORTING HIS DISCIPLES.

LET not your hearts be troubled; ye believe
In God, believe also in Me, His Son.
Doubt not but in the compass of the heavens
My Father will provide for all His saints
Mansions of peace, seats of eternal bliss,
Where spirits made perfect after death shall dwell,
And rest from earthly toils; thither I go
To seal your sure election, and prepare
For you, My faithful servants, an abode
That, as in sorrow here, so there in bliss
With Me, Your Lord, now dying for your sakes,
Ye may surmount the grave, and ever live
In heavenly communion undisturbed.
Lament not, therefore, if I now depart,
Your provident Precursor, for ye know
Whither I go, and also know the way.

CHRIST PASSING OVER KEDRON.

THOU soft flowing Kedron, by thy silver stream,
Our Saviour, at midnight, when Cynthia's pale beam
Shone bright on the waters, would often-times stray,
And lose in thy murmurs the toils of the day.

How damp were the vapors that fell on His head!
How hard was His pillow! how humble His bed!
The angels, astonished, grew sad at the sight,
And followed their Master with solemn delight!

Oh! Garden of Olivet — dear honored spot!
The fame of thy wonders shall ne'er be forgot!
The theme most transporting to Seraphs above,
The triumph of sorrow, the triumph of love.

Come Saints and adore Him, come bow at His feet;
Oh! give Him the glory, the praise that is meet!
Let joyful hosannas unceasing arise,
And join the full chorus that gladdens the skies.

'THE GARDEN OF GETHSEMANÈ.

NIGHT, and the world do rest ! the golden moon,
Bright in her glory, tracks her lumined way ;
And thousand stars at midnight's solemn noon,
Blend soften'd radiance with her shadowy ray :
Hill, glade, and dell, and fountain's flashing spray,
And silvery streamlet glow in chasten'd light,
The night-bird hath awoke her pensive lay
'Mid olive-groves that scale the mountain's height,
And earth doth calmly smile as wrapt in vision bright.

The world doth rest ! Not all—the weary heart
Perchance may sigh o'er pleasure vanishèd ;
Dim eyes may weep 'neath sorrow's ceaseless smart,
Fond bosoms wail the parted and the dead :
For earth hath many a tale of glory fled ;
Her brightest homes have records of deep woe ;
On sweetest blossoms withering blight is shed,
Nor lives for aye youth's fair and spring-time glow,
Joy hath on earth no shrine where sorrow may not flow.

But hither come ! Gethsemanè may speak
Of more than mortal, more than earthly woe !
Ye, ye may tell of hearts that care doth break,
Of fragile forms that hopeless sink below :
Come hither ! God—the God Incarnate know !
A world's deep burden is He doomed to bear !
All guilt, all sorrow, all of man's dark woe,
He, He hath taken to His soul, and there,
Behold Him prostrate laid !—list, list His groaning prayer.

" My Father hear ! if this deep, bitter cup,
This cup of agony untold,—intense,
This cup unmingled with one soothing drop
Of mercy from Thy footstool,—if it hence
May pass away, My Father ! then dispense,
Nor bid Me feel Thy vengeance ! yet if love
Can this permit not, then mine innocence
The weight, the curse of man's offences prove !
Thy will be ever done by all who live and move !"

He ceased,—no voice was heard,—no answer woke
Amid the olive foliage whispering peace ;
No tone from heaven athwart the stillness broke,
To win the sorrowing heart from weariness :
The sad disciples in His last distress
Have yielded to soft slumber, and alone

He wrestles with the Eternal, till the press
Of torturing thought o'erwhelms Him ; yet His moan
Of agony intense hath reach'd the Father's throne.

Again He kneels : "My Father ! if Thy love
Can other means devise,—if this sad cup
May yet pass from Me,—Thou, Thy wrath remove,
Then, then, My Father !—yet if human hope
Doth rest on sacrifice once offer'd up,
And through Thy Son alone the lost may claim
Their full, their free redemption ; then the cup
I take of agony, and woe, and shame,
Thy will, not Mine, be done ! adored Thy glorious name !"

Yet agony hath whelm'd Him ; from His brow
The crimson blood is starting ! low He lies,
But from His lip escapes its burden now—
" Thy will, not Mine, be done ! My sacrifice
Be e'er by Thee accepted !"———

      Lo ! the skies
Their radiant portals open, and a tone.—
A tone angelic, bids the Mourner rise !
And might is given to brave the storm alone !
Salvation's work is wrought ! He bled for man to atone !"

"I DO NOT KNOW THE MAN."

Dost thou not know Me ? hast thou then forgot
The poor lone man by yonder distant sea ?
I call'd and thou didst choose my mournful lot,—
Yes, thou didst leave thy all to follow Me.

Dost thou not know Me ?—Yet this smitten face
Should not be strange to those dim, dazzled eyes,
Which late beheld on Tabor's secret place
The sun, now setting, in such glory rise.

Dost thou not know Me ? Ah, what form had He,
Who, when thy life was sinking in the abyss,
So quickly stretch'd *His* hand to rescue thee !
Look ! *Mine* is bound,—but was that hand like this ?

And can the sheep its bleeding Shepherd smite !
Say, of whose broken body didst thou eat ?
Dost thou not know Me yet ? Who but this night
Knelt down, O my beloved, to wash thy feet ?

In dark Gethsemanè the weight of woe
Press'd drops of blood from this thorn-tortured brow ;—
But ah ! they lead Me to the Cross !—I go ;—
Thou weepest :—tell Me, dost thou know Me *now ?*

THE PASSION OF CHRIST.

Yes ! Thou didst die for me, O Son of God ;
  By Thee the throbbing flesh of man was worn ;
Thy naked feet the thorns of sorrow trod,
  And tempests beat Thy houseless head forlorn :—
    Thou, that wert wont to stand
    Alone, on God's right hand,
Before the ages were, the Eternal, Eldest Born.

Thy birthright in the world was pain and grief ;
  Thy love's return, ingratitude and hate :
The limbs Thou healedst brought Thee no relief ;
  The eyes Thou openedst calmly viewed Thy fate :
    Thou, that wert wont to dwell
    In peace ; tongue cannot tell,
Nor heart conceive the bliss of Thy celestial state.

They dragged Thee to the Roman's solemn hall,
  Where the proud judge in purple splendour sate ;
Thou stood'st a meek and patient criminal,
  Thy doom and death from human lips to wait ;—
    Whose throne shall be the world
    In final ruin hurl'd
With all mankind to hear their everlasting fate.

Thou wert alone in that fierce multitude,
  When "Crucify Him," yelled the general shout ;
No hand to guard Thee 'mid those insults rude,
  Nor lip to bless in all that frantic rout :—
    Whose lightest whispered word
    The adamantine arms from all the heavens broke out.

They bound Thy temples with the twisted thorn ;
  Thy bruisèd feet went languid on with pain ;
The blood from all Thy flesh with scourges torn,
  Deepen'd Thy robe of mockery's crimson grain :
    Whose native vesture bright
    Was the unapproachèd light,
The sandal of whose foot the rapid hurricane.

They smote Thy cheek with many a ruthless palm,
  With the cold spear Thy shuddering side they pierc'd;
The draught of bitterest gall was all the balm
  They gave t' enhance Thy unslak'd burning thirst :—
    Thou, at whose words of peace
    Did pain and anguish cease,
And the long-buried dead their bonds of slumber burst.

Low bow'd Thy head convuls'd and droop'd in death,
  Thy voice sent forth a sad and wailing cry,
Slow struggled from Thy breast the parting breath,
  And every limb was wrung with agony:
    That head, whose veilless blaze
    Filled angels with amaze,
When at that voice sprang forth the rolling suns on high.

And Thou wert laid within the narrow tomb,
  Thy clay-cold limbs with shrouding grave clothes bound.
The sealèd stone confirm'd Thy mortal doom;
  Lone watchmen walk'd Thy desert burial-ground :—
    Whom heav'n could not contain,
    Nor the immeasurable plain
Of vast infinity enclose or circle round.

For us, for us, Thou didst endure the pain,
  And Thy meek spirit bowed itself to shame,
To wash our souls from sin's infecting stain,
  T' avert Thy Father's wrathful vengeance-flame :
    Thou who couldst nothing win,
    By saving worlds from sin,
Nor aught of glory add to Thy all-glorious name.

ECCÈ HOMO.

Oh! sacred head now wounded,
  With grief and scorn weighed down;
Oh! sacred brow—surrounded
  With thorns, Thy only crown!
Once on a throne of glory,
  Adorned with light divine,
Now, all despised and gory;
  I joy to call Thee mine.

Oh! noblest brow, and dearest,
  In other days the world
All feared when Thou appeared'st;

What shame on Thee is hurled!
How art Thou pale with anguish,
　With sore abuse and scorn?
How does that visage languish?
　Which once was bright as morn.

On me, as Thou art dying,
　Oh, turn Thy pitying eye;
To Thee for mercy crying,
　Before the Cross I lie.
Thine, Thine the bitter passion,
　Thy pain is all for me;
Mine, mine the deep transgression,
　My sins are all on Thee.

What language can I borrow,
　To thank Thee—dearest friend;
For all Thy dying sorrow,
　Of all my woes, the end?
Then can I leave Thee ever?
　Oh, do not Thou leave me!
Lord! let me never, never,
　Outlive my love to Thee.

If I, a wretch, should leave Thee,
　Oh! Jesus, leave not me;
In faith may I receive Thee,
　When death shall set me free.
When strength and comfort languish,
　And I must hence depart,—
Release me then from anguish,
　By Thy own wounded heart.

But near me, when I'm dying,
　Oh! show Thy Cross to me;
And for my succor flying,
　Come Lord, and set me free.
This heart, new faith receiving,
　From Jesus shall not rove;
For he who dies believing,
　Dies safely through Thy love.

JUDAS' REPENTANCE.

The morning of the world's great tragedy—
Already shouting crowds cried "Crucify,"
　Around the High Priest's door,
When pressing thro' th' outpouring stream — a man

His eyes with horror fill'd, his features wan,
  Stood breathless on the floor.

"Condemn'd and guiltless!!" gaspingly he said,
" 'Tis I have sinn'd, 'tis I who have betray'd
  The Righteous and the Good.
Take back your bribe with bloody stain,
It burns my hand, it sears my brain,
  Price of my Master's Blood!"

Cold as a hail-storm on the hissing flame,
"See thou to that," the chilling answer came,
  "What matters it to us?"
"Too late! too late!" with frenzi'd voice he cries,
"No justice here, no rescue from the skies,
  "Wretch! to betray Him thus!"

Down from his hand the cursèd coin he cast,
With frantic flying feet the streets he past,
  For burning thro' his brain
From hundred, hundred voices rose the cry,
"Away and crucify Him, crucify
  Again and yet again."

Poor conscience-madden'd wretch! turn even yet,
And throw thyself before thy Saviour's feet,
  His cross take up and bear,
Till thou shalt come to Golgotha, nor leave
Its blood-stained foot till thou a glance receive,
  To save thee from despair.

But no! urg'd onward by the fiends of Hell,
Like those fierce creatures who in tombs did dwell
  And shunn'd the sight of man,
He pass'd Gehenna's drear cursed vale
Where midnight sees fierce Moloch's victims pale
  Gleam in the moonlight wan.

He stay'd not till upon the mountain side
So bleakly grand, so desolately wide
  He for a little stood.
There nature seem'd congenial with despair,
No distant voice upon the lurid air,
  It was the Field of Blood!

When lo! swift blotting out the mid-day sun
Wild chaos seem'd to have again begun
  To desolate the world.
A horror of deep darkness fell around,
Earth trembled to her deepest depths profound,
  Dead from their grave were hurl'd.

The mountains shudder'd and the hills did quake,
The thunders rolling ten-fold echoes wake;
 Where shall the traitor flee?
Hark! thro' the gloom his mad despairing call
"Fall on me rocks, ye tottering mountains fall,
 "And end my misery."

" Ye howling fiends whose curses fill the air
"Not Hell itself can equal my despair,
 " Life — life itself is Hell,
"Yawn! yawn! ye horrid gulfs! Hell open wide
"Within your burning depths my crime I hide."
With one wild spring into the darken'd space
Headlong, rebounding down the rock's steep face
 A mangled corpse he fell.

THE CRUCIFIXION.

City of God! Jerusalem,
Why rushes out thy living stream?
The turbaned priest, the hoary seer,
The Roman in his pride are there!
And thousands, tens of thousands, still
Cluster round Calvary's wild hill.

Still onward rolls the living tide,
There rush the bridegroom and the bride;
Prince, beggar, soldier, Pharisee,
The old, the young, the bond, the free;
The nation's furious multitude,
All maddening with the cry of blood.

'Tis glorious morn;—from height to height
Shoot the keen arrows of the light;
And glorious in their central shower,
Palace of holiness and power,
The temple on Moriah's brow
Looks a new risen sun below.

But woe to hill, and woe to vale!
Against them shall come forth a wail:
And woe to bridegroom and to bride;
For death shall on the whirlwind ride:
And woe to thee, resplendent shrine,
The sword is out for thee and thine.

Hide, hide thee in the heavens, thou sun,
Before the deed of blood is done !
Upon that temple's haughty steep
Jerusalem's last angels weep ;
They see destruction's funeral pall
Blackening o'er Sion's sacred wall.

Like tempest, gathering on the shore,
They hear the coming armies' roar :
They see in Sion's hall of state
The sign that maketh desolate—
The idol—standard—pagan spear,
The tomb, the flame, the massacre.

They see the vengeance fall ; the chain,
The long, long age of guilt and pain :
The exile's thousand desperate years,
The more than groans, the more than tears ;
Jerusalem, a vanish'd name,
Its tribes earth's warning, scoff, and shame.

Still pours along the multitude,
Still rends the heavens the shout of blood,
But on the murderer's furious van,
Who totters on ? a weary Man ;
A cross upon His shoulders bound—
His brow, His frame, one gushing wound.

And now He treads on Calvary,
What slave upon that hill must die ?
What hand, what heart, in guilt imbrued,
Must be the mountain-vulture's food ?
There stand two victims gaunt and bare,
Two culprit emblems of despair.

Yet who the Third ? The yell of shame
Is frenzied at the sufferer's name ;
Hands clenched, teeth gnashing, vestures torn,
The curse, the taunt, the laugh of scorn,
All that the dying hour can sting,
Are round Thee now, Thou thorn-crown'd King !

Yet cursed and tortured, taunted, spurned,
No wrath is for the wrath returned,
No vengeance flashes from the eye ;
The sufferer calmly waits to die :
The sceptre reed, the thorny crown,
Wake on that pallid brow no frown.

At last the word of death is given,
The form is bound, the nails are driven ;
Now triumph, Scribe and Pharisee !

Now, Roman, bend the mocking knee!
The cross is reared. The deed is done.
There stands Messiah's earthly throne!

This was the earth's consummate hour;
For this had blazed the prophet's power;
For this had swept the conqueror's sword,
Had ravaged, raised, cast down, restored;
Persepolis, Rome, Babylon,
For this ye sank, for this ye shone.

Yet things to which earth's brightest beam
Were darkness—earth itself a dream;
Foreheads on which shall crowns be laid,
Sublime, when sun and stars shall fade,
Worlds upon worlds—eternal things—
Hung on Thy anguish, King of kings!

Still from His lip no curse has come,
His lofty eye had looked no doom;
No earthquake burst, no angel brand
Crushes the black, blaspheming band,
What say those lips by anguish riven?
"God, be My murderers forgiven!"

He dies, in whose high victory,
The slayer, death himself, shall die!
He dies! by whose all-conquering tread
Shall yet be crushed the serpent's head;
From his proud throne to darkness hurled,
The god and tempter of this world.

He dies, creation's awful Lord,
Jehovah, Christ, Eternal Word:
To come in thunder from the skies;
To bid the buried world arise;
The earth His footstool, heaven His throne;
Redeemer! may Thy will be done.

THE CRUCIFIXION.

Bound upon th' accursèd tree,
Faint and bleeding, who is He?
By the eyes so pale and dim,
Streaming blood, and writhing limb,
By the flesh with scourges torn,

By the crown of twisted thorn,
By the side so deeply pierced,
By the baffled burning thirst,
By the drooping death-dew'd brow,
Son of Man, 'tis Thou, 'tis Thou!

Bound upon th' accursèd tree,
Dread and awful, who is He?
By the sun at noon-day pale,
Shivering rocks and rending veil,
By earth that trembles at His doom,
By yonder saints who burst their tomb,
By Eden, promised ere He died
To the felon at His side,
Lord! our suppliant knees we bow,
Son of God, 'tis Thou, 'tis Thou!

Bound upon th' accursèd tree,
Sad and dying, who is He?
By the last and bitter cry,
The ghost given up in agony;
By the lifeless body laid
In the chamber of the dead:
By the mourners come to weep
Where the bones of Jesus sleep;
Crucified! we know Thee now;
Son of Man, 'tis Thou, 'tis Thou!

Bound upon th' accursèd tree,
Dread and awful, who is He?
By the prayer for them that slew,
" Lord, they know not what they do!"
By the spoil'd and empty grave,
By the souls He died to save,
By the conquest He hath won,
By the saints before His throne,
By the rainbow round His brow,
Son of God, 'tis Thou, 'tis Thou!

THE CROSS.

No graven image of divinest mould,
No sparkling diamond laid in purest gold,
No crown on any earthly monarch's brow,
To be compared with, Cross of Christ, art thou.
Nimbi of light surround thee, sacred thing,

Mysterious signal of high heaven's King;
Thou brightenest as I gaze, grow, brighten on,
Until He come again, the Judge upon His throne.
Perhaps in farthest zones that boast an orb
To shine the glory of the Creative Word,
The business of mighty Seraphim may be
To search the mystery that lies in thee.
Salvation to the penitent,—what sign
Could still the avenger's awful wrath but thine,
When Cain, the wandering, in the early earth
Was driven an exile from his place of birth?
The King's broad mark, the touch of hands profane
From consecrated things could once restrain.
When Judah's sacred city, gone astray
From God and swerved to each forbidden way,
Was doomed to slaughter, then, as the vision shews,
The murderous weapon glanced aside from those
Upon whose foreheads, by some holy hand,
The wonder-working signal had been *penned*.
Honoured of God and high in human praise,
Through all memorials of the ancient days,
Creation's heroes gloried that they bore thee,
The heavenliest beauties on their white breasts wore thee;
On gilded banners in the dread field of war,
On holy temple tops that gleamed afar,
On rugged cliff and hoary mountain's head,
On antique tombs raised o'er the mighty dead,
Hast thou been lifted up to shew the road
A soul may travel to the blest realms of God.

THE HIGHWAY TO MOUNT CALVARY.

Repair to Pilate's hall, which place when thou hast found,
   There shalt thou see a pillar stand to which thy Lord was
      bound.
'Tis easy to be known by any Christian eye;
   The bloody whips do point it out from all that stand thereby.

A little from that place, upon the left-hand side,
   There is a curious portlie door, right beautiful and wide.
Leave that in any wise, forbid thy foot go thither;
   For out thereat did Judas go, despair and he together.

But to the right-hand turn, where is a narrow gate,
   Forth which St. Peter went to weep his poor distrest estate.
Do imitate the like, go out at sorrow's door,
   Weep bitterly as he did weep, that wept to sin no more.

By this direction, then, the way is understood—
  No porch, no door, nor hall to pass, unsprinkled with Christ's blood.
So shall no error put misguiding steps between,
  For every drop sweet Jesus shed is freshly to be seen.

A crown of piercing thorns there lies imbrued in gore!
  The garland that thy Saviour's head for thy offences wore;
Which when thou shalt behold, think what His love hath been,
  Whose head was laden with those briars t' unload thee of thy sin.

Follow His feet that goes for to redeem thy loss,
  And carries all our sins with Him to cancel on His cross.
Look on with liquid eyes, and sigh from sorrowing mind,
  To see the death's-man go before, the murdering troupes behind.

Then press amongst the throng, thyself with sorrows wed;
  Get very near to Christ and see what tears the women shed;
Tears that did turn Him back, they were of such a force—
  Tears that did purchase daughter's names, of Father's kind remorse.

Think on their force by tears—tears that obtainèd love;
  Where words too weak could not persuade, how tears had power to move.
Then look towards Jesus' load, more than He could endure,
  And how for help to bear the same a hireling they procure.

Join thou unto the cross, bear it of love's desire:
  Do not as Cyrenæus did, who took it up for hire.
The voluntary death that Christ did die for thee,
  Gives life to none but such as joy cross-bearing friends to be.

Up to Mount Calvary if thou desire to go,
  Then take thy cross and follow Christ, thou canst not miss it so.
When thou art there arrived His glorious wounds to see,
  Say but as faithful as the thief, "*O Lord, remember me.*"

Assure thyself to have a gift all gifts excelling,
  Once sold by sin, once bought by Christ, for saints eternal dwelling.
By Adam, Paradise was sin's polluted shade:
  By Christ, the awful Golgotha a Paradise was made.

HYMN FROM THE BREVIARY.

To Christ, the Prince of Peace,
   And Son of God Most High;
The Father of the world to come,—
   Sing we with holy joy.

Deep in His heart for us,
   The wound of love He bore;
That love which still He kindles in
   The hearts that Him adore.

Oh! fount of endless life!
   Oh! spring of fountains clear!
Oh! flame celestial, cleansing all,
   Who unto Thee draw near.

Hide me in Thy dear heart,
   For thither do I fly;
There seek Thy grace through life, in death,—
   Thine immortality.

THE RESURRECTION.

He is risen, He is risen!
   Tell it with a joyful voice,
He has burst his three days' prison,
   Let the whole wide earth rejoice:
Death is conquer'd, man is free,
Christ has won the victory.

Come, ye sad and fearful-hearted,
   With glad smile and radiant brow:
Lent's long shadows have departed,
   All His woes are over now;
And the passion that He bore,
Sin and pain, can vex no more.

Come, with high and holy hymning,
   Chant our Lord's triumphant lay;
Not one darksome cloud is dimming
   Yonder glorious morning ray,
Breaking o'er the purple East;
Brighter far our Easter feast.

He is risen, He is risen !
  He has op'd the eternal gate;
We are free from sin's dark prison,
  Risen to a holier state :
And a brighter Easter beam
On our longing eyes shall stream.

EASTER.

THE TWO MARYS.

Oh dark day of sorrow, amazement and pain;
When the promise was blighted, the given was ta'en !

When the Master no longer a refuge should prove;
And evil was stronger than mercy and love !

Oh dark day of sorrow, abasement and dread,
When the Master beloved was one with the dead !

We sate in our anguish afar off to see,
For we surely believed not this sorrow could be !

But the trust of our spirits was all overthrown;
And we wept, in our anguish, astonished, alone !

At eve they laid Him with aloes and myrrh,
In fine linen wound, in a new sepulchre.

There, there will we seek Him : will wash Him with care;
Anoint Him with spices : and mourn for Him there.

Oh strangest of sorrow ! oh vision of fear !
New grief is around us—the Lord is not here !

THE ANGEL.

Women, why shrink ye with wonder and dread ?—
Seek not the living where slumbers the dead !

Weep not, nor tremble : and be not dismayed;
The Lord hath arisen ! see where He was laid !

The grave-clothes, behold them; the spices; the bier;
The napkin that bound Him; but He is not here !

Death could not hold Him, the grave is a prison
That keeps not the living; the Christ has arisen!

THE LORD JESUS.

WHY are ye troubled? why weep ye and grieve?
What the prophets have written why slowly believe?

'Tis I, be not doubtful! why ponder ye so?
Behold in My body the marks of My woe!

The willing hath suffered; the chosen been slain;
The end is accomplished! behold Me again!

Death has been conquered—the grave has been riven—
For sin a remission hath freely been given!

Fearless in spirit, yet meek as the dove,
Go preach to the nations this gospel of love.

For the might of the mighty shall o'er you be cast;
And I will be with you, my friends, to the last.

I go to the Father, but I will prepare
You mansions of glory, and welcome you there.

There life never ending; there bliss that endures;
There love never changing, My friends, shall be yours!

But the hour is accomplished, My children, we sever—
But be ye not troubled, I am with you for ever!

JOURNEY TO EMMAUS.

It happened on a solemn eventide
Soon after He that was our Surety died,
Two bosom friends, each pensively inclined,
The scene of all those sorrows left behind,
Sought their own village, busied as they went
In musings worthy of the great event:
They spake of Him they loved, of Him whose life,
Though blameless, had incurred perpetual strife;
Whose deeds had left, in spite of hostile arts,
A deep memorial graven on their hearts.
The recollection, like a vein of ore

The further traced, enriched them still the more;
They thought Him, and they justly thought Him, one
Sent to do more than He appeared t' have done:
To exalt a people and to place them high
Above all else, and wondered He should die.
Ere yet they brought their journey to an end,
A stranger joined them, courteous as a friend,
And asked them, with a kind engaging air,
What their affliction was, and begged a share.
Informed, He gathered up the broken thread,
And, truth and wisdom gracing all He said,
Explained, illustrated, and searched so well
The tender theme on which they chose to dwell,
That reaching home, "The night," they said, " is near,
We must not now be parted—sojourn here."
The new acquaintance soon became a guest,
And made so welcome at their simple feast,
He blessed the bread, but vanished at the word,
And left them both exclaiming, " 'Twas the Lord!
Did not our hearts feel all He deigned to say?
Did they not burn within us by the way?"

THE ASCENSION.

Bright portals of the sky,
Embossed with sparkling stars;
Doors of eternity,
With adamantine bars:
Your arras rich uphold,
Loose all your bolts and springs;
Ope wide your leaves of gold,
That in your roofs may come the King of kings!

Scarfed in a rosy cloud,
He doth ascend the air;
Straight doth the moon Him shroud
With her resplendent hair.
The next encrystalled light
Submits to Him its beams;
And He doth trace the height
Of that fair lamp which flames of beauty streams.

He towers those golden bounds,
He did to sun bequeath;
The higher wandering rounds
Are found His feet beneath.
The milky-way comes near,

Heaven's axle seems to bend
Above each turning sphere,
That, robed in glory, Heaven's King may ascend.

Oh ! well-spring of this all !
Thy Father's image *vive*;
Word—that from nought did call,
What is—doth reason—live !
The soul's eternal food,
Earth's joy—delight of Heaven ;
All truth, love, beauty, good,
To Thee, to Thee, be praises *ever* given

Now each etherial gate
To Him hath opened been ;
And glory's King in state
His palace enters in.
Now come is this High Priest,
In this most holy place ;
Not without blood addressed,
With glory heaven, the earth to crown with grace.

Oh ! Glory of the heaven !
Oh ! Sole Delight of earth !
To Thee all power be given ;
God's uncreated birth.
Of mankind lover true,
Endurer of his wrong ;
Who dost the world renew,
Still be Thou our salvation and our song.

THE ASCENSION.

Our Lord is risen from the dead,
 Our Jesus is gone up on high ;
The powers of hell are captive led,
 Dragg'd to the portals of the sky.
There His triumphant chariot waits,
 And angels chant the solemn lay ;
Lift up your heads, ye heavenly gates,
 Ye everlasting doors give way.

Loose all your bars of massy light,
 And wide unfold the etherial scene ;
He claims these mansions as His right,
 Receive the King of Glory in.

Who is the King of Glory ? who ?
　　The Lord who all our foes o'ercame ;
　　The world, sin, death, and hel o'erthrew,
　　And Jesus is the Conqueror's name.

Lo ! His triumphant chariot waits,
　　And angels chant the solemn lay :
Lift up your heads ye heavenly gates,
　　Ye everlasting doors give way !
Who is the King of Glory ? who ?
　　The Lord of glorious power possess'd ;
　　The King of saints and angels too,
　　God over all, forever blessed.

WHITSUNTIDE, OR PENTECOST.

When God of old came down from heaven,
　　In power and wrath He came ;
Before His feet the clouds were riven,
　　Half darkness and half flame :

But when He came the second time,
　　He came in power and love ;
Softer than gale at morning prime
　　Hover'd His holy Dove.

The fires, that rush'd on Sinai down
　　In sudden torrents dread,
Now gently light, a glorious crown,
　　On every sainted head.

And as on Israel's awe-struck ear
　　The voice exceeding loud,
The trump, that Angels quake to hear,
　　Thrill'd from the deep, dark cloud ;

So, when the Spirit of our God
　　Came down His flock to find,
A voice from heaven was heard abroad,
　　A rushing, mighty wind.

It fills the Church of God ; it fills
　　The sinful world around ;
Only in stubborn hearts and wills
　　No place for it is found.

Come Lord, come Wisdom, Love, and Power,
　Open our ears to hear ;
Let us not miss the accepted hour ;
　Save, Lord, by love or fear.

ST. STEPHEN THE PROTO-MARTYR.

As rays around the source of light,
Stream upward ere he glow in sight,
And watching by his future flight,
　　Set the clear heaven on fire ;
So on the King of Martyrs wait
Three chosen bands in royal state,
And all earth owns—of good and great—
　　Is gathered in that choir.

One presses on, and welcomes death,
One calmly yields his willing breath,—
Nor slow, nor hurrying, but in faith,
　　Content to die or live ;
And some, the darlings of their Lord,
Play smiling with the flame and sword,
And, ere they speak to His sure word,
　　Unconscious witness give.

Foremost and nearest to His throne,
By perfect robes of triumph known,—
And likest Him in look and tone,
　　The holy Stephen kneels ;
With steadfast gaze as when the sky
Flew open to His fainting eye,
Which, like a fading lamp, flashed high,—
　　Seeing what death conceals.

Well might you guess what vision bright
Was present to his raptured sight,
Even as reflected streams of light,
　　Their solar source betray ;
The glory which our God surrounds,
The Son of Man—th' atoning wounds—
He sees them all ; and earth's dull bounds
　　Are melting fast away.

He sees them all—no other view
Could stamp the Saviour's likeness true,
Or with His love so deep embrue

Man's sullen heart and gross—
" Jesus, do Thou my soul receive ;
Jesus, do Thou my foes forgive ; "
He who would learn that prayer, must live
    Under the holy Cross.

He, though He seems on earth to move,
Must glide in air like gentle dove,
From yon unclouded depths above
    Must draw His purer breath ;
Till men behold His angel face
All radiant with celestial grace,
Martyr all o'er, and meet to trace
    The lines of Jesus' death.

ST. STEPHEN THE PROTO-MARTYR.

A COUNCIL-ROOM in old Jerusalem
Is filled with eager faces. Men who feel
The blood of Abraham in their veins are there,
Some born 'neath Sion, others from afar,
(In Africa, in Asia, and in Rome,
Long held in bondage) suffered to return,
To worship in the city of their God,
To pray for their deliverance that should come
By Him whom all the prophets prophesied.
He came—unto His own ; they knew Him not,
And the glad tidings that He brought they scorned.
He left them with a self-imposèd curse
On them and on their children. Even now,
That curse is growing to accomplishment
In that doomed city ; soon, no stone shall rest
Upon another, in its holiest place.
The meek, the lowly, loving Man of Griefs
Wept over it with keenest sympathy,
Such as no human heart e'er felt before.
His words of peace they heard not, nay, they mocked,
Reviled and buffeted and spat upon,
Condemned and crucified the King of kings.

So came, so died the Saviour of the world.
Only a few of all the favoured seed
Of Abram, who beheld the Son of God,
Believed on Him and worshipped ; and to these,
His seed, the travail of His soul, He gave
The promise of His presence to " the end, "
" I will not leave you orphans, I will send
Another Comforter."

                    With sorrowing eyes,
The true desciples saw the gates of death
Close on their Lord and Master. But He rose
Triumphant from the grave, and they beheld
His well-loved form once more and heard Him speak,
In words that made their hearts within them burn,
" Go forth beginning at Jerusalem,
And preach remission of their sins to men."
He blessed them, and the opening clouds received
His body from their sight.
                    They were alone—
Not long ; the promise given was fulfilled ;
The Spirit came : the Heavenly Comforter,
Proceeding from the Father and the Son,
Who taught them all things, filled their souls with joy,
And gave them strength and courage to declare
That Christ had suffered for a guilty world.

And many souls were added to the Church
Of such as should be saved. These kept the Faith,
Through toils and persecution, scorn and shame.
Jerusalem, that crucified her King,
Jerusalem that shed the prophet's blood,
Still thirsted, and insatiate asked for more—
Now, in that council-room with craving eyes
They look upon their prey. His face is bright,
As is an angel's, whom the smile of God
Has lightened with the glory of His love.
But ah ! those eyes had seen the Son of God,
In all His awful agony undimmed.
His death and resurrection Stephen preached.
Full of the Holy Spirit, faith and power,
And many miracles and wonders wrought,
Convincing sinners of the Truth he spake,
Till even priests themselves obeyed the Faith.

    Then wicked men arose, and with hard words,
Disputed Stephen's. Vainly they withstood,
Celestial wisdom hovered round his lips.
Then, full of rage and falsehood they suborned
Men, like themselves, unprincipled, who said
That Stephen had blasphemed the holy place,
The law, and Moses who had given it.
And the high-priest demanded a reply—
Are these things so ? But Stephen, undismayed
By all that proud tribunal's scorn and hate,
Spake boldly as the Spirit moved his lips,
Beginning with the father of their race,
His call, his promise of posterity,
His prompt obedience, his unshaken faith,
He told them all their sinful history,

Their disobedience, their ingratitude,
Their base idolatry. How through all their sin,
God still was with them, and by prophets spake
Of Him the Just One, that should come to save
His chosen people Israel, from their sins,
Yea, all the world, if they would but believe ;
And how they slew those prophets, and at last,
(The consummation of their heinous sin)
Betrayed and murdered Him they had foretold ;—
And as their fathers did, so did they still.
He ceased. His words had cut them to the heart,
And full of demon rage they gnashed their teeth :

But he had spoken only words of love ;
Dove-like, his indignation had no gall.
He boldly spoke the truth to save their souls.
For this he was ordained and sent to preach,
That all might feel the deadly weight of sin,
And look to Christ that He might give them rest.
He had borne fearless witness to the Truth
Amidst its enemies ; and not in vain,
For 'midst those enemies was *one* whom God
Had chos'n for high and holy purposes,
Who afterwards remembered all his words,
The martyr-seed was sown in goodly soil.

He ceased, and looking steadfastly to heaven,
Beheld God's glory inexpressible,
And Jesus Christ standing at God's right hand.

He told his vision. They impenitent,
And tenfold more filled with demoniac rage,
Smothered his voice with cries and stopped their ears,
And rushed with one accord, a fiendish crowd,
Upon their victim, and with murderous force,
Cast him without the city, and with stones,
(Meet emblems of their hardened hearts) they slew
Stephen with *crowned* king-martyr of the Cross.
" That they might be forgiven for their sins,"
Was his last prayer ;—and so he fell asleep.

SAINT PETER IN PRISON.

Thou thrice denied, yet thrice beloved,
    Watch by Thine own forgiven friend ;
In sharpest perils faithful proved,
    Let his soul love Thee to the end.

The prayer is heard—else why so deep
   His slumber on the eve of death?
And wherefore smiles he in his sleep
   As one who drew celestial breath?

He loves and is beloved again —
   Can his soul choose but be at rest?
Sorrow hath fled away, and pain
   Doth not invade the guarded nest.

He dearly loves, and not alone,
   For his winged thoughts are soaring high—
Where never yet frail heart was known
   To breathe in vain affection's sigh.

He loves and weeps—but more than tears
   Have sealed Thy welcome and his love—
One look lives in him, and endears
   Crosses and wrongs where'er he rove.

That gracious tending look, Thy call
   To win him to himself and Thee;
Salute the sorrow of his fall,
   Which else were ru'd too bitterly.

Even through the veil of sleep it shines,
   The memory of that kindly glance;
An angel, watching by, divines,
   And spares awhile, his blissful trance.

Or haply, to his native lake,
   His vision wafts him back to talk
With JESUS, ere his flight he take,
   As in that solemn evening walk,

When to the bosom of his friend,
   The Shepherd, He whose name is Good,
Did His dear lambs and sheep commend,
   Both bought and nourished with His blood.

Then laid on him th' inverted tree,
   Which, firm embraced with heart and arm,
Might cast o'er hope and memory,
   O'er life and death, its awful charm.

With lightening heart he bears it on,
   His passport through th' eternal gates
To his sweet home—so nearly won,
   He seems, as by the door he waits—

The unexpressive notes to hear
　Of angel song and angel motion,
Rising and falling on the ear,
　Like waves in joy's unbounded ocean.

His dream is changed—the Tyrant's voice
　Calls to that last of glorious deeds—
But as he rises to rejoice,
　No Herod, but an angel leads.

He dreams he sees a lamp flash bright,
　Glancing around his prison room—
But 'tis a gleam of heavenly light
　That fills up all the ample gloom.

The flame, that in a few short years,
　Deep through the chambers of the dead
Shall pierce, and dry the fount of tears,
　Is waving o'er his dungeon-bed.

Touched, he upstarts—his chains unbind—
　Through darksome vault, up massy stair,
His dizzy, doubting footsteps wind,
　To freedom and cool midnight air.

Then all himself, all joy and calm,
　Though for a while his hand forego;
Just as it touched the Martyr's palm,
　He turns him to his task below.

The pastoral staff, the keys of Heaven,
　To wield awhile in grey-haired might;
Then from his cross to spring forgiven,
　And follow JESUS out of sight.

THE CONVERSION OF SAINT PAUL.

The mid-day sun, with fiercest glare,
Broods o'er the hazy, twinkling air,
　Along the level sand;
The palm-trees, shade unwavering lies,
Just as thy towers, Damascus, rise,
　To greet yon wearied band.

The leader of that martial crew
Seems bent some mighty deed to do,
　So steadily he speeds;

With lips firm closed, and fixèd eye,
Like warrior when the fight is nigh,
   Nor talk nor landscape heeds.

What sudden blaze is round him poured,
As though all heaven's refulgent hoard
   In one rich glory shone?
One moment—and to earth he falls:
What voice his inmost heart appals?
   Voice heard by him alone.

For to the rest both words and form
Seem lost in lightning and in storm,
   While Saul in wakeful trance—
Sees deep within that dazzling field
His persecuted Lord revealed,
   With keen, yet pitying glance;

And hears the meek, upbraiding call
As gently on his spirit fall,
   As if th' Almighty Son
Were prisoner yet on this dark earth,
Nor had proclaimed His royal birth,
   Nor His great power begun.

"Ah! wherefore persecut'st thou Me?"
He heard and saw, and sought to free
   His strained eye from the sight;
But heaven's high magic bound it there,
Still gazing, though untaught to bear
   Th' unsufferable light.

"Who art Thou, Lord?" he falters forth:
So shall sin ask of heaven and earth
   At the last awful day:
"When did we see Thee suffering nigh,
And passed Thee with unheeding eye,
   Great God of Judgment Day?"

Ah! little dream our listless eyes,
What glorious presence they despise,
   While in our room of life;
To power or fame we rudely press—
Christ is at hand to scorn or bless,
   Christ suffers in our strife.

And though heaven's gates long since have closed,
And our dear Lord in bliss reposed,
   High above mortal ken;
To every ear in every land
(Though meek ears only understand),
   He speaks as He did then.

"Ah! wherefore persecute ye Me?
'Tis hard ye so in love should be
 With your own endless woe;
Know, though at God's right hand I live,
I feel each wound you reckless give
 To the least saint below."

" I in your care, My brethren, left,
Not willing ye should be bereft
 Of waiting on your Lord;
The meanest offering ye can make —
A drop of water — for love's sake,
 In heaven, be sure, is stored."

Oh! by those gentle tones and dear,
When Thou hast stayed our wild career,
 Thou only hope of souls;
Ne'er let us cast one look behind,
But in the thought of Jesus find
 What every thought controls.

As to Thy last Apostle's heart
Thy lightning glance did then impart,
 Zeal's never-dying fire;
So teach us on Thy shrine to lay
Our hearts, and let them day by day,
 Intenser blaze, and higher.

And as each mild and winning note
(Like pulses that round harp-strings float
 When the full strain is o'er),
Left lingering on his inward ear,
Music that taught, as death drew near,
 Love's lesson more and more.

So, as we walk our earthly round,
Still may the echo of that sound
 Be in our memory stored;
"Christians! behold your happy state,
Christ is in those who on Him wait!
 Make much of your dear Lord!"

THE SECOND ADVENT.

Thou art the King of Glory, blessèd Lord!
 The Father's everlasting Son;
Eternally the co-existent Word:

And now, for victories won
In human flesh, Thee all the heavens adore,
Who at the Father's right hand reignest evermore.

All power in heaven and earth Thou wieldest there,
    The Lord of Hades and of death,
The keys of that dark empire Thou dost bear,
    O'er all things that have breath,
Thy rule extends, by hell in vain opposed :
Thou openest, none can shut nor force what Thou hast closed.

Not yet are all things put beneath Thy feet;
    Not yet the kingdoms of this world
Are Thine; nor yet, consummate his defeat,
    The Prince of Darkness hurled
Down into hell's unfathomable void,
Nor Death, man's final foe, with Eerth's dark king, destroyed.

But Heaven and Earth and Hell, or with glad zeal
    Or blind concurrence, work thy will.
The day that shall the perfect scheme reveal,
    And all Thy word fulfil,
Is drawing on; and Farth is ripening fast
As for the sickle. Soon shall sound that signal blast.

We know that Thou art coming, mighty Lord !
    To be the judge of quick and dead ;
To give thy faithful servants their reward :
    To crush the Serpent's head :
Lord, in Thy merits and Thy grace unbounded
1 put my trust; O let me never be confounded.

THE SECOND ADVENT.

EVEN thus, amid thy pride and luxury,
O earth ! shall that last coming burst on thee,
    That secret coming of the Son of Man,
When all the cherub-throning clouds shall shine
Irradiate with His bright advancing sign :
    When that great Husbandman shall wave His fan,
Sweeping like chaff, thy wealth and pomp away :
Still in the noon-tide of that nightless day,
    Shalt thou thy wonted dissolute course maintain.
Along the busy mart and crowded street,
The buyer and the seller still shall meet,
    And marriage feasts begin their jocund strain :

Still to the pouring out the cup of woe;
Till earth, a drunkard, reeling to and fro,
And mountains molten by His burning feet,
And heaven His presence own, all red with furnace heat.

  The hundred-gatèd cities then,
  The towers and temples, named of men
   Eternal and the thrones of kings;
  The gilded summer-palaces,
  The courtly bowers of love and ease,
   Where still the bird of pleasure sings;
  Ask ye the destiny of them?
  Go, gaze on fallen Jerusalem!
Yea, mightier names are in the fatal roll,
'Gainst earth and heaven God's standard is unfurl'd,
The skies are shrivelled like a burning scroll,
 And the vast common doom ensepulchres the world.

  Oh! who shall then survive?
  Oh! who shall stand and live?
  When all that hath been is no more:
   When for the round earth hung in air,
   With all its constellations fair
    In the sky's azure canopy;
When all the breathing earth, and sparkling sea,
 Is but a fiery deluge without shore,
Heaving along the abyss profound and dark,
A fiery deluge and without an ark.
  Lord of all power, when Thou art there alone,
  On Thy eternal, fiery wheelèd throne,
   That in its high meridian noon
   Needs not the perished sun or moon:
When Thou art there in Thy presiding state,
 Wide-sceptered monarch o'er the realm of doom,
When from the sea-depths, from earth's darkest womb
The dead of all the ages round Thee walk;
And when the tribes of wickedness are strown,
 Like forest leaves in th' autumn of Thine ire:
Faithful and true! Thou still wilt save Thine own!
 The saints shall dwell within th' unharming fire,
Each white robe spotless, blooming every palm,
  Even safe as we, by this still fountain side,
 So shall the Church, Thy bright and mystic Bride,
Sit on the stormy gulf, a halcyon bird of calm.
  Yes, 'mid yon angry and destroying signs,
  O'er us the rainbow of Thy mercy shines;
We hail, we bless the covenant of its beam,
Almighty to avenge, almightiest to redeem!

THE TWO HORSEMEN.

1st PART.

He cometh! He cometh! the death-dealing king,
His pale steed is fleet as the hurricane's wing;
Around Him are ravening the monsters of hell,
Earth shrinks from their aspect, and shakes with their yell.

He cometh! He cometh! with sword dripping gore:
Desolation behind Him, and terror before:
His banner of darkness above Him is spread,
With pestilent vapour earth smokes at His tread.

Her kings and her captains oppose Him in vain;
Her mantle no longer can cover her slain;
The great are down-trampled, the mighty ones fail,
And their armies are scattered like leaves on the gale.

The beasts of the forest exult o'er their prey,
Grim Slaughter mows onward his merciless way,
Gaunt Famine, and livid Disease, at His side,
O'er monarchs and nations triumphantly ride.

And now from their slumber the tempests awaken:
They rage, and the stars from their orbits are shaken;
The sun gathers blackness, the moon turns to blood,
The heavens pass away; and the isles from the flood,

And the mountains from earth, at the tumult retreat:
The prince and the peasant—the abject, the great—
The youthful, the agèd—the fearful, the brave—
The strong man, the feeble—the freeman, the slave,

To caverns and dens for a hiding-place run;
But who the keen eye of Jehovah can shun?
From His face to conceal them, despairing they call
To the rocks and the mountains upon them to fall:

In vain; for the day of decision at last
Has dawned, and the season of mercy is past:
He cometh from heaven, with the sword and the rod,
Who shall tread in His fury the wine-press of God.

His angel the fowls is inviting aloud
To the carnage of steeds and their riders to crowd,
Whose flesh shall be mangled, whose blood shall be spilled,
That the vultures and ravens may eat and be filled.

2ND PART.

He cometh! He cometh! how glorious the sight!
His horse as the snow newly fallen is white;
On His head are the crowns that betoken His power,
From His eyes flash red lightnings His foes to devour.

In blood has the vesture been dipped that He wears,
And a name on His thigh and His vesture He bears;
The Sovereign of sovereigns, that loftiest of names,
The Lord of all lords, its possessor proclaims.

And white are the horses, as now without stain,
Of the thousands of thousands who ride in His train;
And white and unspotted the robes He has given
To be worn on this day by the armies of heaven.

The bow in His hand, lo! unerring He bends,
With the sword from His mouth every spirit He rends,
By His rod are down smitten all they that oppose,
And from conquering to conquer resistless He goes.

But see, where His presence the darkness illumes,
How lovely the aspect creation assumes!
New heavens, a new earth, a new ocean arise,
That fill every heart with a welcome surprise.

A city majestic and spacious appears,
Which sin cannot enter, where dried are all tears;
With beauty resplendent, from dangers secure;
Where fruits are perennial, and waters as pure

As He who erects it, the blessèd await:
With shoutings of triumph they enter the gate,
With God, their Redeemer, for ever to reign,
And it closes on all, but the Lamb and His train.

THE LAST DAY.

The day of wrath, that dreadful day,
When heaven and earth shall pass away!
What power shall be the sinner's stay?
How shall he meet that dreadful day?

When, shriv'lling like a parchèd scroll,
The flaming heavens together roll,
And louder yet, and yet more dread,
Swells the high trump that wakes the dead.

Oh! on that day, that wrathful day,
When man to judgment wakes from clay,
Be Thou, O Christ! the sinner's stay,
Though heaven and earth shall pass away.

THE FINAL JUDGMENT.

This done, the Omnipotent, Omniscient Judge,
Rose, infinite, the sentence to pronounce—
The sentence of eternal love or bliss !
All glory heretofore seen or conceived ;
All majesty annihilated, dropped
That moment from remembrance, and was lost ;
And silence, deepest hitherto esteemed,
Seemed noisy to the stillness of this hour.
Comparisons I seek not, nor should find,
If sought : that silence which all being held
When God Almighty's Son from off the walls
Of heaven the rebel angels threw, accursed,
So still, that all creation heard them fall
Distinctly in the lake of burning fire,
Was now forgotten, and every silence else.
All being rational, created, then
Around the judgment seat, intensely listened ;
No creature breathed : man, angel, devil, stood
And listened ; the spheres stood still and every star
Stood still and listened ; and every particle
Remotest in the womb of matter, stood
Bending to hear, devotional and still.
And then upon the wicked first, the Judge
Pronounced the sentence written before of old :
" Depart from Me, ye curs'd, into the fire
Prepared eternal in the gulf of Hell,
Where ye shall weep and wail for evermore,
Reaping the harvest which your sins have sown."
      * * * * * *

This done, the glorious Judge turning to right
With countenance of love unspeakable,
Beheld the righteous, and approved them thus :
" Ye blessèd of My Father, come ; ye just,
Enter the joy eternal of your Lord;
Receive your crowns, ascend and sit with Me,
At God's right hand in glory evermore."

THE SONG OF THE HUNDRED AND FORTY AND FOUR THOUSAND.

Who are these in bright array,
This innumerable throng,
Round the altar night and day,
Hymning one triumphant song?
"Worthy is the Lamb once slain,
Blessing, honour, glory, power,
Wisdom, riches, to obtain,
New dominion every hour."

These through fiery trials trod,
These from great affliction came;
Now before the throne of God,
Seal'd with His almighty name;
Clad in raiment pure and white,
Victor-palms in every hand,
Through their dear Redeemer's might,
More than conquerors they stand.

Hunger, thirst, disease unknown,
On immortal fruits they feed;
Them, the Lamb amidst the throne,
Shall to living fountains lead:
Joy and gladness banish sighs,
Perfect love dispels all fears,
And for ever from their eyes,
God shall wipe away the tears.

THE PLEASURES OF HEAVEN.

There all the happy souls that ever were,
Shall meet with gladness in one theatre;
And each shall know there one another's face,
By beatific virtue of the place.
There shall the brother with the sister walk,
And sons and daughters with their parents talk;
But all of God: they still shall have to say,
But make Him all in all their theme that day;
That happy day that never shall see night!
Where He will be all beauty to the sight;

Wine or delicious fruits unto the taste;
A music in the ears will ever last;
Unto the scent, a spicery or balm;
And to the touch, a flower, like soft as palm.
He will all glory, all perfection be,
God in the Union and the Trinity!

That holy, great, and glorious mystery,
Will there revealèd be in majesty,
By light and comfort of spiritual grace;
The vision of our Saviour face to face,
In His humanity! to hear Him preach
The price of our redemption, and to teach,
Through His inherent righteousness in death
The safety of our souls and forfeit breath!
What fulness of beatitude is here!
What love with mercy mixèd doth appear!
To style us friends who were by nature foes!
Adopt us heirs by grace, who were of those
Had lost ourselves; and prodigally spent
Our native portions and possessèd rent!
Yet have all debts forgiven us; an advance
By imputed right to an inheritance
In His eternal kingdom, where we sit
Equal with angels, and co-heirs of it.

THE BETTER LAND.

" I HEAR thee speak of the better land;
Thou call'st its children a happy band:
Mother! oh where is that radiant shore?—
Shall we not seek it, and weep no more?
Is it where the flower of the orange blows,
And the fire-flies dance through the myrtle boughs?"
 " Not there, not there, my child!"

" Is it where the feathery palm trees rise,
And the date grows ripe under sunny skies?
Or 'midst the green islands of glittering seas,
Where fragrant forests perfume the breeze,
And strange, bright birds, on their starry wings,
Bear the rich hues of all glorious things?"
 " Not there, not there, my child!"

" Is it far away, in some region old,
Where the rivers wander o'er sands of gold ?—
Where the burning rays of the ruby shine,
And the diamond lights up the secret mine,
And the pearl gleams forth from the coral strand ?—
Is it there, sweet mother, that better land ?"
　　" Not there, not there, my child ! "

" Eye hath not seen it, my gentle boy!
Ear hath not heard its deep songs of joy ;
Dreams cannot picture a world so fair,—
Sorrow and death cannot enter there;
Time doth not breathe on its fadeless bloom,
For, beyond the clouds, and beyond the tomb,
　　It is *there*, it is *there*, my child ! "

THE CITY OF REST.

O BIRDS from out the east, O birds from out the west,
Have ye found that happy city in all your quest ?
Tell me, tell me, from earth's wandering may the heart find
　　glad surcease ?
Can ye show me as an earnest any olive branch of peace ?
I am weary of life's troubles, of its sin, and toil, and care :
I am faithless, crushing in my heart so many a fruitless prayer.
O birds from out the east, O birds from out the west,
Can ye tell me of that City the name of which is Rest ?

Say, doth a dreamy atmosphere that blessèd city crown ?
Are there couches spread for sleeping softer than the eider
　　down ?
Does the silver sound of waters falling 'twixt its marble walls,
Hush its solemn silence even into stiller intervals ?
Doth the poppy shed its influence there, or doth the fabled
　　moly
With its leafy-laden Lethè lade the eyes with slumber holy ?
Do they never wake to sorrow, who after toilsome quest,
Have entered in that City the name of which is Rest ?

Doth the fancy wile not there for aye ? Is the restless soul's
　　endeavour
Hushed in a rhythm of solemn calm, forever and forever ?
Are human natures satisfied of their intense desire ?
Is there no more good beyond to seek, or do they not aspire ?
But weary, weary of the ore within its yellow sun,

Do they lie and eat its lotus leaves, and dream life's toil is
  done?
O tell me, do they there forget what here hath made them
  blest?
Nor sigh again for home and friends in the City namèd Rest?

O little birds, fly east again,—O little birds, fly west;
Ye have found no happy city in all your weary quest,
Still shall ye find no spot of rest wherever ye may stray,
And still like you the weary soul must wing its weary way;
There sleepeth no such city within the wide earth's bound,
Nor hath the dreaming fancy yet its blissful portals found.
We are but children crying here upon a mother's breast,
For life and peace and blessedness, and for Eternal Rest?

Bless God, I hear a still, small voice, above life's clamorous
  din,
Saying, faint not, thou weary one, thou yet may'st enter in;
That City is prepared for those who well do win the fight,
Who tread the wine-press till its blood hath washed their gar-
  ments white.
Within it is no darkness, nor any baleful flower
Shall there oppress thy weeping eyes with stupefying power,
It lieth calm within the light of God's peace-giving breast,
Its walls are called SALVATION, the City's name is REST.

THE END.

TABLE OF CONTENTS.

PART I.

HISTORICAL INCIDENTS OF THE OLD TESTAMENT.

                                                                                                              PAGE.

The Creation	Addison	5
The Creation	Milton	6
The First Sabbath	Do	7
God Visible in all Nature	Cowper	8
Adam's First Sensations	Milton	9
The Garden of Eden	Do	10
Eve's Recollections	Do	11
Eve to Adam	Do	12
"Adam, Where Art Thou?"	Ragg	12
Adam and Eve leaving Paradise	Milton	14
Eve's First Born	Mrs. Sigourney	14
"Cain, Where is Thy Brother Abel?"	Ragg	15
Cain on the Sea-Shore	Stolberg	16
"Enoch walked with God"	Mrs. Hemans	18
The Deluge	Proctor	19
Subsiding of the Waters of the Deluge	Milton	21
To the Rainbow	Campbell	21
The Destruction of Sodom	Croly	23
Abraham's Sacrifice	Mrs. Leprohon	24
Hagar and Ishmael	Anon	25
Abraham at Machpelah	Mrs. Sigourney	27
The Repentance of Esau	A. M. B. V.	28
Jacob's Dream	Croly	29
Jacob Wrestling with the Angel	Wesley	30
The Burial of Jacob	J. D. Burns	32
The Finding of Moses	Grahame	34
Jochebed's Soliloquy	Hannah More	35
The Seventh Plague of Egypt	Croly	36
The First-Born of Egypt	Anon	38
The Passage of the Red Sea	Heber	40
The Song of Miriam	Edmeston	42
Balaam	Anon	43
Sisera	Reade	44
Jephthah	Do	44
Jephthah's Daughter	Byron	45
Samson's Lament for the Loss of his Sight	Milton	46
Hannah and Samuel	Mrs. Hemans	47
The Child Samuel	J. D. B.	49
David and Goliath	Drummond	50
Saul and David	Grahame	53

TABLE OF CONTENTS.

		PAGE.
Saul in the Cave of Engedi	Heavysege	53
Saul and the Witch of Endor	Byron	54
The Three Mighty Men	Anon	55
David's Lamentation over his Sick Child	N. P. Willis	57
Absalom	Do	60
Temples	Darnell	62
Elijah's Interview	Campbell	63
Elisha	Anon	64
The Destruction of Sennacherib	Byron	65
Choral Hymn of the Jewish Maidens	Milman	66
Jerusalem	Moore	68
Palestine	Heber	69
Hymn of the Captive Jews	Milman	70
Oh! Weep for Those	Byron	71
On Jordan's Banks	Do	71
Hymn of the Hebrew Maid	Scott	72
"By the Waters of Babylon."	McGee	72
Ariel	Anon	73
Nehemiah	Do	74
The Messiah	Pope	75
The Repentance of Nineveh	Anon	78
Babylon is Fallen	Do	79
The Cities of Old	Brownlee	80
Tyre	Mary Howitt	82
The Fall of Nineveh	Anon	83
The Vision in the Valley of Dry Bones	Do	85
Belshazzar	Byron	86
Belshazzar's Feast	T. S. Hughes	87
Daniel's Soliloquy	Hannah More	90
Daniel's Prophecy—the Fall of Babylon	Do	90
The Maccabees	McGee	91
A Hebrew Melody	Hogg	93
Watchman! what of the Night?	Bowring	94

PART II.

HISTORICAL INCIDENTS OF THE NEW TESTAMENT.

		PAGE.
Messiah's Advent	Anon	97
Advent	Do	89
Saint John the Baptist	Drummond	100
A Prelude for Christmas	McGee	100
The Annunciation of the Blessèd Virgin Mary	Keble	102
Hymn on the Nativity	Mrs. Hemans	104
A Bethlehem Hymn	Bonar	104
Bethlehem	McDuff	105
Christ's Nativity	Campbell	106
A Christmas Carol	E. H. Seers	107
Carol	Anon	108
Christmas	Do	109
Adeste Fideles	Do	110

TABLE OF CONTENTS.

		PAGE.
The Incarnation	Milman	111
Christmas Day	Keble	112
The Madonna and Child	Dale	113
The Stable at Bethlehem	Mrs. Leprohon	114
The Epiphany; or, Manifestation of Christ to the Gentiles	Heber	115
The Star of Bethlehem	Cowper	116
The Holy Innocents	Keble	117
Rachel weeping for her Children	Heber	118
The Presentation of Christ in the Temple	Mrs. Leprohon	119
The Purification of the Blessèd Virgin	Keble	120
Our Saviour's Boyhood	Mrs. Leprohon	121
Christ in the Wilderness	Milton	122
The Fasting	Anon	123
Christ Performing Miracles	Taylor	124
Saint John the Baptist Beheaded	E. H. Bickersteth	125
The Leper	N. P. Willis	133
The Widow of Nain	Heber	136
The Widow of Nain	Dale	138
Mary Magdalene	Darnell	138
The Memorial of Mary	Mrs. Hemans	140
The Night in Galilee	Reade	140
Christ Stilling the Tempest	Anon	141
The Raising of the Daughter of Jairus	N. P. Willis	142
The Raising of the Daughter of Jairus	Doane	143
The Woman of Canaan	Newton	144
The Transfiguration	Anon	145
The Ten Lepers	Mrs. Leprohon	146
Lazarus	Adeline	147
The Raising of Lazarus	Dale	151
Christ Blessing Little Children	Julia Gill	152
Christ Blessing Little Children	Mrs. Sigourney	153
Christ's Entry into Jerusalem	Croly	155
Christ's Entry into Jerusalem	Milman	156
Christ Weeping over Jerusalem	Dale	156
Christ Comforting His Disciples	Cumberland	157
Christ Passing over Kedron	Marie De Fleury	157
The Garden of Gethsemanè	Adeline	158
"I do not know the Man"	Anon	159
The Passion of Christ	Milman	160
Eccè Homo	Paul Gerhardt	161
Judas' Repentance	A. M. B. V.	162
The Crucifixion	Croly	164
The Crucifixion	Milman	166
The Cross	Leach	167
The Highway to Mount Calvary	Anon	168
Hymn from the Breviary	Do	170
The Resurrection	Do	170
Easter	Mary Howitt	171
Journey to Emmaus	Cowper	172
The Ascension	Drummond	173
The Ascension	Anon	174
Whitsuntide, or Pentecost	Do	175

TABLE OF CONTENTS.

		PAGE.
Saint Stephen the Proto-Martyr	Keble	176
Saint Stephen the Proto-Martyr	Reade	177
Saint Peter in Prison	Keble	179
The Conversion of Saint Paul	Do	181
The Second Advent	Condor	183
The Second Advent	Milman	184
The Two Horsemen	Greenwood	186
The Last Day	Scott	187
The Final Judgment	Pollock	188
The Song of the Hundred and Forty and Four Thousand	Montgomery	189
The Pleasures of Heaven	Jonson	189
The Better Land	Mrs. Hemans	190
The City of Rest	Hymns of the ages	191

www.ingramcontent.com/pod-product-compliance
Lightning Source LLC
Chambersburg PA
CBHW032130160426
43197CB00008B/579